THE ENCYCLOPEDIA OF

Kitchen Tools

THE ENCYCLOPEDIA OF

Kitchen Tools

◇

ESSENTIAL ITEMS FOR THE HEART OF YOUR HOME—AND HOW TO USE THEM

Elinor Hutton

BLACK DOG
& LEVENTHAL
PUBLISHERS
NEW YORK

Black Dog & Leventhal Publishers
Hachette Book Group
1290 Avenue of the Americas
New York, NY 10104

www.hachettebookgroup.com
www.blackdogandleventhal.com

First Edition: October 2020

Black Dog & Leventhal Publishers is an imprint of Perseus Books, LLC,
a subsidiary of Hachette Book Group, Inc. The Black Dog & Leventhal
Publishers name and logo are trademarks of Hachette Book Group, Inc.

The publisher is not responsible for websites (or their content) that are
not owned by the publisher.

The Hachette Speakers Bureau provides a wide range of authors for
speaking events. To find out more, go to www.HachetteSpeakersBureau.com
or call (866) 376-6591.

Print book interior design by Joanna Price

LCCN: 2020933088

ISBNs: 978-0-7624-6998-7 (hardcover), 978-0-7624-9730-0 (ebook)

Printed in China

1010

10 9 8 7 6 5 4 3 2 1

Contents

INTRODUCTION

The Encyclopedia of Kitchen Tools comprises 300 of the most common and most obscure pieces of cooking equipment found in Western kitchens. From the largest appliances to the smallest gadgets, and many things in between, this guide explains what each tool is, how it works, and how to put it to good culinary use. Divided into five large sections—including the best prep gear to make your food, and all the necessary tableware required to serve it—the entries have been alphabetized and split into subcategories as needed.

Please note that the organized sections of this book are meant to help collect like-minded tools into groups, but they are subjective classifications.

For example, the cake turntable (page 98) is found in the Kitchen Accessories section, but could easily and rightfully be classified in Baking and Decorating Tools. Be sure to reference this book's two indexes if you cannot locate an entry. To help with ease of location, we've provided one index that organizes each item alphabetically, and a second index that organizes each item by use.

Above all, know that each of these kitchen tools was created to make life in the kitchen easier or more productive. Learn about what they can do, lean on their help, and enjoy your time cooking!

—Elinor Hutton

APPLIANCES

Cookers & Fryers

The age of electric self-supervising cooking machines is now. There are a variety to choose from, all with different capabilities, and some of which are able to do almost everything. Because the cook can often "set it and forget it" (a tagline from a popular cooker in the 1990s), some of these machines are especially helpful for time-crunched home cooks. Using a countertop fryer does not save any time, but it certainly limits some of the dangers and mess associated with more traditional methods.

AIR FRYER

Often marketed as a healthier alternative to deep-frying, an air fryer is a countertop kitchen appliance that circulates warm air around a food to mimic the crispy and browned exterior one achieves in deep-frying. To use an air fryer, add whatever ingredient is to be "fried" to the rack in the fryer after coating or spraying the food with a nominal amount of oil. Then, once the lid has been closed, hot air circulates around the food, allowing it to cook. While the end result is not quite the same as a traditionally fried food (and is in fact quite similar to that of a food cooked on a rack in a convection oven), the final product is appealing enough that the air fryer remains a popular alternative—or, at least, a novel alternative—to standard frying.

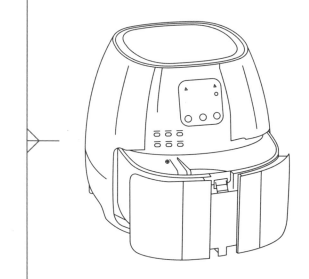

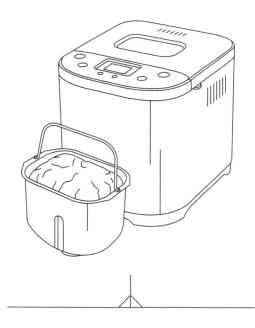

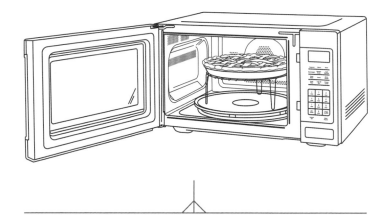

BREAD MACHINE

Instead of mixing, kneading, proofing, and baking bread by hand, one can simply add raw ingredients directly to a bread machine, select a program, walk away, and return later to a finished loaf. The electric countertop machine includes a main compartment, where one adds the ingredients and retrieves the finished bread; the internal machinery includes parts that mix, knead, and proof the dough, as well as a heating component for baking. Because of the fixed size of the section of the machine where the bread is baked, only a fixed shape loaf can be produced; one cannot bake rolls, baguettes, or other shapes.

CONVECTION MICROWAVE

A convection microwave is a cross between a convection oven (page 46) and a microwave (page 47); it is able to combine the speed of a microwave with the power of a convection oven, which relies on a fan to circulate hot air. The benefit of this combination is that food is able to cook or heat through quickly using the microwave functionality, but at the same time, can be browned and crisped in the circulating heat provided by the convection function. (Microwaves are usually unable to brown or crisp on their own; see browning dish, page 68.) This countertop electric appliance is often built into a home kitchen like a microwave, and current versions come equipped with digital controls.

DEEP FRYER

Available in both a small countertop version meant for home cooks, or a giant, stand-alone industrial version made for commercial kitchens and restaurants, and everything in between, a deep fryer is an appliance that, obviously, deep-fries foods. Consisting of a vessel that heats and holds cooking oil at a constant temperature along with a fitted basket that aids in the lowering and lifting of ingredients, a deep fryer works in the same manner as a pot of oil on the stovetop: by submerging food into hot oil and cooking it until it is rendered crispy and brown. As opposed to stovetop frying, using a deep fryer consumes less energy and is more easily monitored for temperature. Additionally, by providing an option for frying that allows cooks to move away from the flames of a gas range, deep fryers produce a safer cooking environment that can mean fewer accidents.

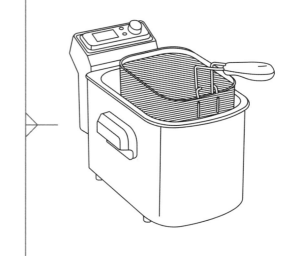

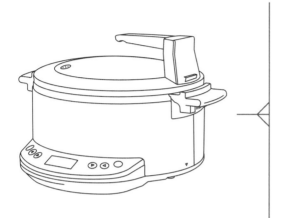

MULTICOOKER

A multicooker is a cooking appliance comprising a cylindrical metal vessel and a hinged, fitted lid, which is able to perform a variety of cooking functions, depending on the setting and accessory chosen. These abilities can include rice cooking, steaming, slow cooking, pressure cooking, yogurt making, and more, all of which do not require supervision, as the machine includes a timer and shut off capabilities. A popular brand of multicooker is the Instant Pot.

POPCORN MAKER/AIR POPPER

A popcorn maker is a single use electric appliance meant for popping corn. While making popcorn on the stovetop remains a pretty simple act, only an air popper, a particular type of popcorn machine, can pop kernels without added oil; otherwise, the maker simply offers an easier way to make popcorn, via the convenience of an automated machine. The air popper contains a heating element and a fan; when the kernels get hot enough, they pop, jumping into a separate cooling container where they are held until ready to be dispensed. Other types of popcorn machines heat oil inside an enclosed canister; the corn kernels pop when they hit the oil.

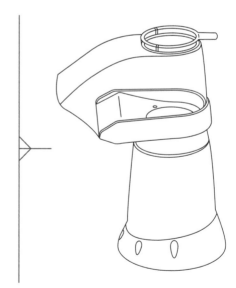

PRESSURE COOKER

A pressure cooker is a specialized pot or countertop appliance that cooks food in a pressurized environment, significantly speeding up the cooking time of the food contained inside. The original stovetop version of a pressure cooker includes a pot and a locking lid with a pressure release valve and a pop-up pressure indicator; the appliance version has a similar main vessel and lid, but comes with digitally automated controls and is heated via electricity rather than by the stovetop. Both versions work in the same way: by heating the sealed pot, a pressurized environment is created, which raises the boiling point of water, forcing ingredients and the liquid surrounding them to cook faster.

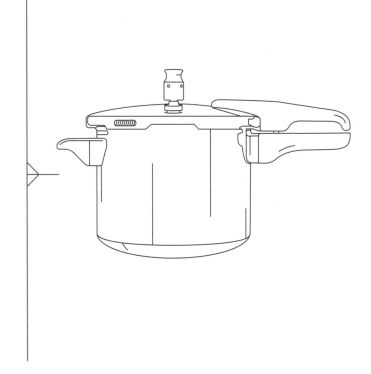

Under Pressure

Pressure cookers have been around for centuries and are especially popular in bean and pulse (lentils, peas, chickpeas, etc.) eating cultures, like India, as they significantly speed up preparation times for these staples. They have recently become more mainstream in the US, due to the proliferation of multicookers that include this function. While these pots (and their cousins the pressure canner and the pressure fryer) are all safe when used properly, care is still required to avoid dangerous accidents. Read (and reread) instructions and be vigilant regarding volume limits and pressure release procedures.

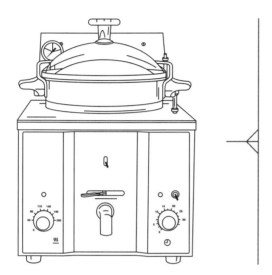

PRESSURE FRYER

A stand-alone industrial appliance found almost entirely in commercial kitchens, a pressure fryer adheres to the standard deep-frying process but it performs this process in an airtight, pressurized environment. Similar to a pressure cooker (opposite page) but absolutely not a substitute, a pressure fryer uses a special, self-contained vessel to hold the food and the oil and adds pressure, which raises the boiling point of water (found in the food to be fried). This results in a quicker cook time and a juicier end result.

The Secret to Success

Pressure fryers were not a popular piece of equipment when Harland Sanders stumbled upon this unique option for frying chicken. Unhappy with the amount of time it took to shallow fry a piece of bone-in chicken on the stovetop, Sanders experimented with frying chicken in a pressure fryer. The newfangled cooking method was a success, as is the Colonel's now-global brand of franchise restaurants, Kentucky Fried Chicken.

RICE COOKER

A rice cooker is an electric appliance specially made to cook rice. Containing a vessel made to hold the raw rice and water, and often coated in a nonstick substance, the rice cooker has a lid, a valve that releases excess steam, and manual or digital controls to turn the machine on and off. More advanced machines offer greater functionality, such as automatic shut off, specialized settings that keep contents warm, or the ability to cook other grains, such as bulger, millet, and quinoa. Additional accessories are also available, including a steamer basket, which can be suspended above the cooking rice to cook vegetables or fish.

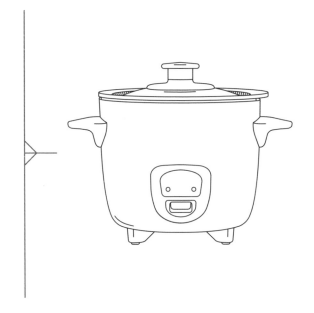

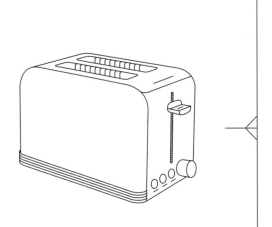

SLOT TOASTER

A slot toaster is a small appliance used for toasting bread. One adds the bread, often sliced or halved, to the toaster vertically and presses down on a lever that lowers the bread into the slot while simultaneously turning the machine on. The two interior planes of the slot are made of vertical electric coils that heat up to toast the bread as it sits suspended between them. Slot toasters can have a single slot or multiple slots, able to accommodate several slices of bread at once. Some models have extra wide slots which allow them to hold thicker breads and even bagels. As opposed to a toaster oven (page 49), which is horizontally oriented, the slot toaster should not be used to toast bread with any toppings, as the vertical orientation all but guarantees that these toppings will slide off and burn.

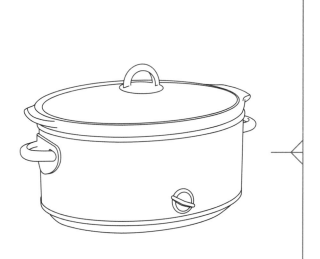

SLOW COOKER

A slow cooker is a countertop appliance with a large vessel for food and a tempered glass lid that is able to generate and maintain a particular cooking temperature thanks to an internalized heating implement. Most slow cookers have two settings, high and low, both of which cook food at a relatively low temperature for an extended period of time (usually about four hours on high, or eight hours on low). The slow cooker is intended to make "low-and-slow" cooking easy—cooking tough cuts of meat, dried beans, or stews—largely unattended (often while the cook sleeps or is at work). Additional functionalities, like an automatic shut off or warming setting (to hold or gently reheat food), are common.

STEAM COOKER

Similar to a rice cooker, a steam cooker, also known as a food or vegetable steamer, is a machine that cooks the contents of its enclosed vessel using steam heat. Usually consisting of transparent, stacked compartments situated over a base that supplies the steam, the steam cooker is then able to cook multiple items at once.

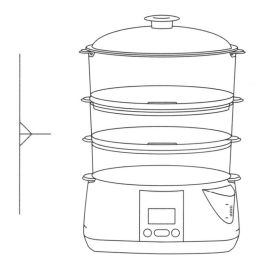

Drink Makers

CARBONATOR

COFFEEMAKER

ELECTRIC KETTLE

ESPRESSO MACHINE

JUICER

PERCOLATOR

Drinks have their own specialized set of tools and appliances made specifically to manipulate water—by heating or carbonating, for example—or to create beverages like juice, coffee, and tea.

CARBONATOR

Also called a soda maker or seltzer maker, a carbonator is an appliance which injects pressurized carbon dioxide, compressed in a canister, into water to create seltzer. To use, a specialized bottle is screwed into the machine to make an airtight seal, and a quick pump or push of a button forces the pressurized CO_2 from the attached canister into the bottle via a nozzle. The pressure is then released and the carbonated bottle of water is removed and ready to drink.

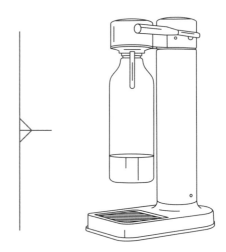

The Best Seltzer

To get the fizziest seltzer, use a carbonator to inject CO_2 into already cold water. Cold water is able to hold more of the injected gas than warm water, resulting in a fizzier drink.

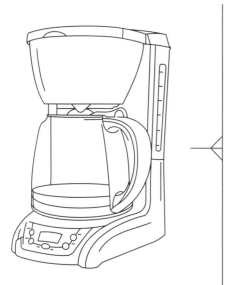

COFFEEMAKER

A countertop appliance common in many households, a coffeemaker—sometimes called a drip coffeemaker, as opposed to a percolator (page 25)—makes coffee by dripping hot water over coffee grounds and catching the brewed coffee as it filters through. Designs vary, but most coffeemakers include a basket that holds a coffee filter (sometimes the basket, if made of mesh, functions as its own filter) and a carafe, or pot of some sort, to catch the finished coffee; there is also a heating element that will both heat the water used to brew the coffee and also keeps the finished coffee warm. Some models are outfitted with the ability to program a start time and an automatic shut off, allowing users to pre-fill their coffeemakers and wake up to a ready-to-drink brew.

ELECTRIC KETTLE

An electric kettle is a glass or metal pot or canister that heats water using electricity. The countertop appliance is helpful for making tea or filter coffee, or for boiling water for cooking. Its appeal is that is does not use the stovetop, which saves fuel (though it does use electricity), and can boil water very quickly.

ESPRESSO MACHINE

An espresso machine is a countertop appliance that makes espresso. Commercial versions and home models function similarly, driven by either steam, a piston, or a pump to create pressure inside the machine. This pressure is applied to water, which is forced through finely ground roasted coffee beans that have been tamped down into a dense puck, to create a strong and concentrated espresso. Machines vary greatly in size and attachments; one common addition is a wand that steams milk, convenient for making lattes.

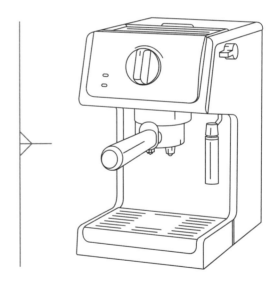

Espresso Machines vs. Coffee Machines

Espresso and coffee are both liquids created from ground roasted coffee beans. The main difference stems from the environment in which the water and beans meet. As opposed to a coffee maker, which uses the relatively gentle pull of gravity to filter the water through the grounds, an espresso machine filters pressurized water through the grounds more forcefully and quickly. An espresso machine also uses hotter water than a coffee machine, allowing the espresso machine to extract different flavor compounds.

JUICER

While one can use a citrus squeezer (page 208) or reamer (page 207) for acquiring small amounts of juice from lemons, limes, or oranges, a juicer is the best option for extracting the juice out of a wider variety of fruits and vegetables, and in larger quantities. There are two main types of this countertop electric appliance: a masticating juicer and a centrifugal juicer. The masticating juicer uses an auger to crush the fruits and vegetables and extract their juice. This is a slower process, but it's one that does not produce any heat (hence the term "cold-pressed"), allowing for the retention of more temperature-sensitive nutrients and enzymes. The centrifugal juicer chops the ingredients and uses centrifugal force to extract the juice from the pulp; this process is faster, but does not extract as much juice as the masticating version. The centrifugal juicer also creates heat, possibly harming some of the sensitive properties of the juice.

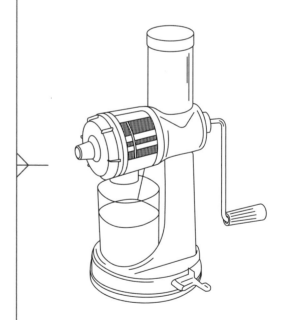

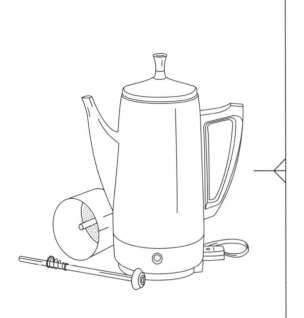

PERCOLATOR

A percolator is an appliance that brews coffee, often using electricity. To use it, fill the bottom of the canister with water, insert the accompanying filter (a perforated metal bowl) filled with ground coffee beans, and close the lid, then plug the entire apparatus into a wall outlet. As the water in the canister becomes hot, it is forced upward through a vertical tube that then distributes it on top of the grounds. The water then filters through the grounds and down into the original chamber of the canister. The liquid coffee continues this cycle, getting stronger as time passes, until the appliance is turned off. Though typically operated via electric power, there are percolators that have been made to be placed directly over a heat source, such as a gas stovetop or a campfire, thereby eliminating the need for an electric power source.

Coffee Culture

There are multiple coffee brewing apparatus that have become popular in recent years. A Chemex is a coffee pitcher that has an inverted cone-shaped top that holds a filter for ground coffee; water is then poured over slowly and repeatedly. A French press holds grounds and hot water together in a vessel until a filter plunger is pressed down to separate the ground beans from the finished coffee; the finished coffee is then simply poured out. A Moka filter is an Italian percolator designed especially for espresso, and used on top of the stove. A pour-over filter is simple and direct—a filter sits on your pitcher or mug and is filled with ground coffee; water is then poured over the coffee grounds and the mug collects the finished brew.

Grills & Griddles

BARBEQUE GRILL

CREPE MAKER

FLATTOP GRILL

GRIDDLE

SANDWICH GRILL/

PANINI MAKER

WAFFLE IRON

Grills and griddles are appliances that have a horizontal cooking surface, either flat or with ridges or bars. While a barbeque grill is used outside, many of the others are countertop appliances meant for single use, like making waffles or crepes.

BARBEQUE GRILL

A barbeque grill, sometimes called just a grill or barbeque, is an outdoor cooking appliance, typically fueled by either gas (via a portable gas tank) or charcoal. Designs vary and range from very simple to highly complex, but all include space for the live fire (sometimes called a firebox), which is usually elevated for safety and convenience, as well as a rack or grates for the food to cook on, and a vented lid. Gas grills are heated by multiple burners, distributing the heat below the entire rack. To start the fire on a grill of this type, the gas line needs to be opened and the flames lit with either an ignition switch, a lighter, or a match. A charcoal grill requires a fire to be started in the well of the grill; when the coals ash over, cooking can begin.

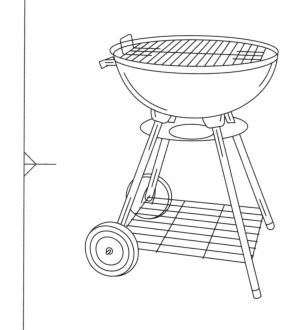

Adding Versatility to Your Charcoal Grill

With a charcoal grill, it can be difficult to control the amount of heat you are subjecting food to, as the rack is usually fixed into place. One method for controlling heat is to arrange the coals in a variety of ways to offset the direct heat and create a space that is cooler. A popular arrangement is a two-zone fire, where hot coals are piled only on one side of the grill. In this case, place food above the coals for direct searing, and then for cooler, indirect roasting, baking, or finishing, move the food to the side of the rack without any coals beneath and cover with the lid.

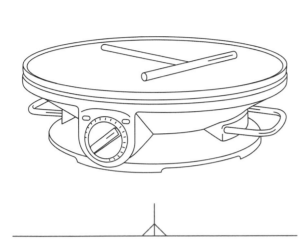

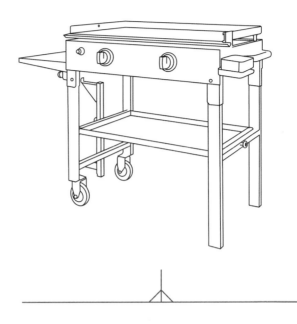

CREPE MAKER

A crepe maker is a circular electric countertop griddle specifically designed for making crepes. The surface plate of a crepe maker is usually made of aluminum or cast iron, and is often treated with a nonstick coating to aid with removal of the delicate crepe once it is cooked. A crepe maker often comes with a wooden spreader and spatula that help to evenly disperse the batter over the cooking surface. Most models also include temperature controls and a timer, which help to ensure even and precise cooking.

FLATTOP GRILL

A flattop grill is a type of cooktop appliance that consists of multiple, circular heating elements situated beneath a permanent, continuously flat cooking surface. This method of circular, radial heating creates an extremely hot, and evenly dispersed, cooking surface. Another bonus of the flattop grill is the material used to fabricate the surface. Made of metal, a flattop grill can be both cooked upon directly, or used with pots and pans, like a range. Since it does not include grates, the food that is cooked directly on the flattop does not drain any fat or juices. Most often used in restaurants, especially diners, a flattop is wonderful for cooking short-order type food, like eggs, pancakes, and burgers.

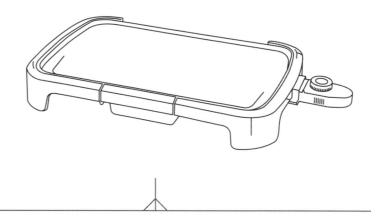

GRIDDLE

Broadly, a griddle is a flat cooking surface, and comes in a variety of forms, either as a freestanding appliance, a portable electric countertop appliance, or as a type of pan or covering that sits above the burners of a gas stove or open fire. The surface of a griddle is usually made of aluminum, carbon steel, or stainless steel, and in electric countertop versions, it is often treated with a nonstick coating. Older, traditional griddles have been constructed of brick, stone, clay, or metals. As opposed to a grill, which has grates that drain food as it cooks and exposes the food to more direct heat and smoke, a griddle contains the food and its juices as it cooks. Unlike a flattop grill, a griddle appliance uses a rectangular heating element, which creates hotter zones and cooler zones on the surface—this can be useful if you are cooking a variety of things that require different temperatures. In addition, a griddle is only meant to be used as a direct cooking surface, and cannot accommodate pots and pans.

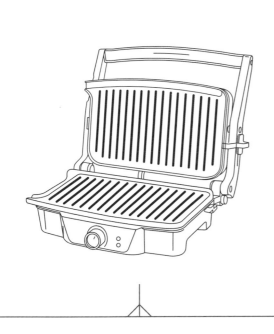

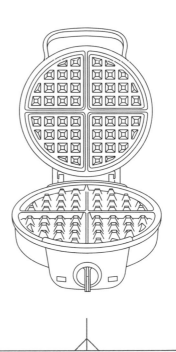

SANDWICH GRILL/PANINI MAKER

A sandwich grill, also known as a panini maker, is an electric countertop press that contains two metal plates which compress a sandwich and toast it at the same time. The bottom plate sits horizontally (or slightly tilted down, to drain), and the top plate swings open and closed on a hinge. When closed, the top plate should sit parallel to the bottom plate. When the metal plates, often coated in a nonstick coating, are hot, a sandwich is nestled inside, and the weight of the top plate presses down on it, compressing it slightly as it cooks. The end result is a thinner sandwich with a crispy exterior and a hot, gooey interior—if cheese has been added, it melts. Though the grill is intended to be used for making sandwiches (*panini* in Italian), many other items can be cooked on it, including chicken cutlets, vegetables, bacon, and even crostini. A very popular version of the sandwich grill was made by George Foreman.

WAFFLE IRON

A waffle iron is an appliance that sandwiches together two fitted, square-dimpled metal plates that work to mold formless batter into waffles. After preheating the iron, waffle batter is poured into the bottom plate, filling all of its concavities, then the iron is closed on its hinge, sealing the batter inside, and flipped over. Once the iron is flipped, gravity pulls the batter on the interior of the appliance down to the second plate. After it cooks for the allotted time (a timer is usually included), the lid of the waffle iron is lifted and a cooked waffle is removed. Originally, waffle irons were non-electric and consisted of two hinged cast iron plates that were heated on the stovetop. Though still in use, these prototypical waffle irons are far less common than their newfangled electric siblings.

Kitchen Appliances

FREEZER

REFRIGERATOR

Arguably, the two of the most important appliances in the kitchen are the refrigerator and freezer. Because of the artificially cold temperatures, food stays fresh longer, making it possible to stock up on ingredients ahead of time and cook them as needed.

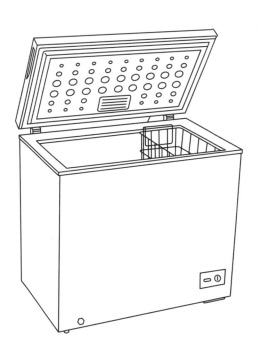

FREEZER

A freezer is an insulated box meant to keep its contents at or below 0°F. If packaged correctly, food placed in the freezer has a much longer life, often up to a few months. This appliance is standard in most Western kitchens and comes in a variety of styles, though most often a freezer comes attached to a refrigerator (opposite page), making one large two-part appliance; styles vary from freezers that sit inside the refrigerator (this style is less common now than it was before 2000), to freezers that stack below or beside the refrigerator. Inside, a freezer will often include a network of shelves, drawers, and compartments that help keep food organized. The freezer can also stand alone as a single appliance. A chest freezer is a particularly large type of freezer that opens from the top and is often placed outside of the kitchen, in a less trafficked area such as a garage or basement. Popular among hunters, fishermen, larger families, and breastfeeding mothers, a chest freezer can hold things at an even colder temperature and offers longer term storage. One popular special feature found in most modern freezers is an icemaker, which automatically molds and collects ice cubes.

REFRIGERATOR

The refrigerator is an insulated box with a cooling element that is meant to keep its contents at around 40°F. A must-have appliance in Western kitchens, a refrigerator is often included in the basic kitchen set-up, along with a stovetop (page 48) and oven (page 47). The inside of the fridge, as it's known colloquially, has various drawers, compartments, and shelves for storing food and beverages, and is accessed by a door that seals shut. Though commonplace in modern kitchens, the refrigerator has drastically changed the way various cultures prepare and store food. Before the refrigerator's existence, food preservation meant utilizing cooking techniques such as smoking, curing, and pickling; for example, the lack of refrigeration made milk inevitably prone to spoilage, and thus created entire categories of food like cheese and yogurt, which change the form of milk to preserve it longer at warmer temperatures. Also, refrigerators enable people to keep food fresh longer, making it possible to shop for food less; cultures without consistent refrigeration acquire food daily, and only in quantities that they can consume within a day or two at most—a less efficient process. Standalone fridges of various sizes exist, and many have a freezer (opposite page) attached, either inside, alongside, or below the refrigerator itself.

Mixing & Blending

BLENDER

FOOD PROCESSOR

HAND MIXER

ICE CREAM MAKER

IMMERSION BLENDER

SPICE GRINDER

STAND MIXER

Due to the force needed to blend and chop by hand, these appliances arguably make the best use of their electric source of energy—they complete laborious tasks in a matter of minutes, sometimes in seconds. While each of these appliances has its specialty, ranging from chopping to blending to whipping, many are relatively multipurpose and may be used to accomplish a variety of kitchen duties.

BLENDER

Used to mix, pureé, liquify, or blend ingredients, a kitchen blender is a tall electronic appliance made up of a set of small rotating blades positioned at the bottom of a glass pitcher. Blenders are most often used for liquid mixtures like sauces, smoothies, and pureed soups; the design of the pitcher and blades creates a vortex when turned on, which captures and blends liquid much better than solids. Because the blades are always found at the base of the pitcher, some versions include a wand that can be safely inserted into the pitcher to help push the contents toward the bottom to reach the blades.

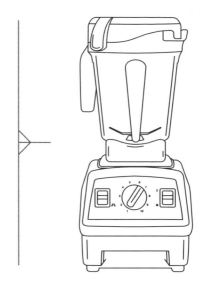

Design Secrets

Blenders are often used for liquid-based mixtures like sauces or marinades. As such, most blenders include specific design features that make this appliance especially adept at performing its duties. When making mayonnaise or hollandaise sauce, the oil or melted butter is meant to be dribbled in very slowly, so that the mixture emulsifies. The blender is designed to help. The lid of a blender often has a detachable cap covering a small opening in the middle of the lid. With the cap removed, it is possible to pour liquids into the machine safely as it runs.

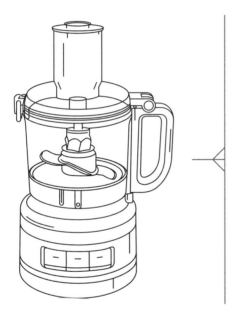

FOOD PROCESSOR

A food processor is a countertop appliance that uses various rotating blade attachments to chop, slice, blend, and pulverize ingredients. Most versions include a plastic bowl, much wider than the ptcher of a blender, that is mounted onto a motor which powers the rotating of the blade. The lid of the plastic bowl includes an open tube so foods can be added to the bowl of the machine while it is running; this also acts as a feeding tube for the slicing blade. In addition to turning on and off, a food processor also spins the blade momentarily, or "pulses," which gives the operator the ability to process ingredients to a lesser degree, like chopping peanuts without making them into peanut butter.

HAND MIXER

A hand mixer is a handheld electric appliance consisting of a pair of motorized, rotating beaters or whisks that are attached to a handle and then maneuvered around a bowl of ingredients. Attachments for a hand mixer are best used for blending and incorporating air into soft ingredients; for example, creaming together sugar and butter, whipping cream, and blending batters, doughs, and frostings. Controls that allow the user to regulate the attachments' speed are built into the mixer's handle. The close access of these additional controls is helpful in the mixing and blending process of especially delicate tasks, when the difference between light and airy egg whites and overbeaten egg whites can be a matter of seconds.

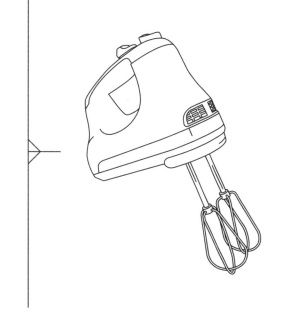

Differentiating Between Mixers and Processors

Most cooks will not need every type of mixing machine. When choosing which machine is right for the job at hand, consider the amount of control each machine offers, what degree of mixing and processing is required, which attachment is needed, and the amount of product being processed. While a blender and food processor use blades to work their ingredients, a handheld mixer and a stand mixer use either beaters or whisks to accomplish their tasks. An immersion blender can be inserted into a jar or pot, while a stand mixer has a large bowl of its own. These differences make each appliance uniquely positioned to execute certain tasks, while also limiting their abilities in some respects.

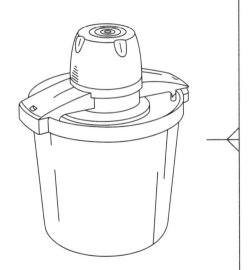

ICE CREAM MAKER

An ice cream maker is an appliance that freezes custard and fruit purees and turns them into ice creams and sorbets. These appliances can take a few different forms, though all include a bowl that holds the liquid mixture and a paddle that churns the mixture. On the higher end is an electric machine containing a compressor that freezes the mixture as well as a motor to spin the paddle and churn the mixture. The most common version is an electric option that does not include a compressor, making it necessary to freeze the work bowl ahead of time so that it can chill the mixture with its residual temperature; this version does churn the mixture automatically. A third option is the original ice cream machine, which must be cranked by hand and is, therefore, less common. This archetypal option works using either a pre-chilled bowl, or a room temperature work bowl that is suspended inside of a larger container which, in turn, is filled with ice and salt to lower the temperature of the bowl. Once everything is in place, the paddle is manually and continuously cranked to stir the ice cream as it freezes. In all versions, the paddle's movements work to churn and aerate the mixture, keeping it smooth and discouraging the formation of large ice crystals.

IMMERSION BLENDER

Also called a stick blender, an immersion blender is a vertically oriented handheld machine with a small rotating blade on one end. Functionally, it has the same abilities as a blender, but does not have its own vessel; instead the blade end is inserted into the container of the food that needs to be blended. This mobility makes an immersion blender wonderfully convenient for blending soups right in the pot, a task that would otherwise require ladling multiple batches into a standard blender. An immersion blender is also great for mixing smoothies, pesto, and salad dressings.

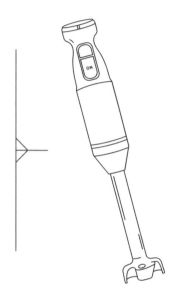

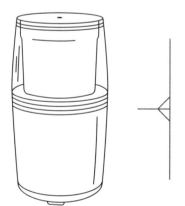

SPICE GRINDER

While manual spice grinders exist (like a larger version of a pepper mill, page 221), the electric version is much more common these days. With a small rotating blade, the spice grinder can process hard spices, such as whole peppercorns, fennel seeds, etc., into various degrees of fineness.

Spice Grinding Alternatives

Spice grinders are very similar to coffee grinders, and if you take care to clean between uses, a coffee grinder can be a fine substitute, negating the need for two very similar machines. However, some chefs and cooks say that grinding spices in a mortar and pestle (page 199) is better than any machine, as crushing the spices, as opposed to cutting them, releases more of their essential oils and gives the cook more control over the grind.

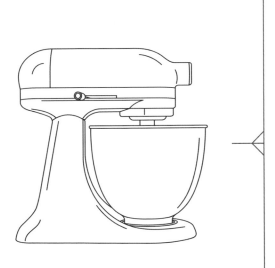

STAND MIXER

A stand mixer is the largest of all mixing appliances. A typical stand mixer consists of an extra-large glass or metal work bowl, a substantial base on which the bowl sits, and an arm attached to the base that hangs horizontally over the work bowl. This arm can hold various mixing attachments that will beat, whisk, and knead the contents of the bowl. The arm also includes controls that allow the user to regulate the speed of mixing. Like a hand mixer (page 40) but stronger, this machine is best for whipping air into mixtures (like cream or egg whites), blending together stiffer mixtures like frostings and cookie dough, and kneading bread or pizza dough. Some stand mixers also come with more esoteric attachments that allow users to grind meat, spiralize vegetables, and roll pasta.

Ovens & Stoves

CONVECTION OVEN

HOT PLATE

MICROWAVE OVEN

OVEN

RANGE/STOVE

STOVETOP/COOKTOP

TOASTER OVEN

Stoves are generally defined as in-home appliances that are used to cook food, whether by burning fuel (gas, wood, charcoal, or the like) or by consuming electricity. In first-world countries, most stoves include a cooktop/stovetop and an oven, though they can be separated by design. This combination of stovetop and oven can also be called a range. Confusingly, many shorten the word *stovetop* to *stove*, losing the distinction between the full appliance and the horizontal cooking.

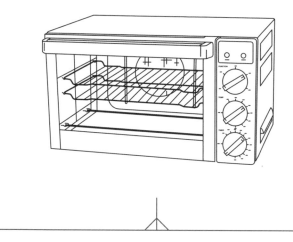

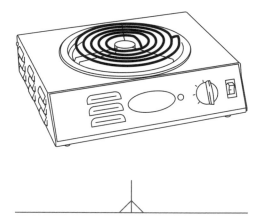

CONVECTION OVEN

A convection oven is either a built-in oven or a small countertop appliance, which must include a special feature: a small fan or other mechanism that circulates hot air, and a vent through which steam is removed. These simple additions to an otherwise conventional oven can drastically alter cooking times and temperatures. Foods cooked in a convection oven are cooked through more quickly and evenly as the hot air is blowing directly on them, and because the vent removes the humid air, a drier cooking environment is created, which is more optimal for browning. This makes certain tasks, like roasting a chicken, much easier and convenient. However, other more delicate tasks, like making a souffle, become troublesome. It is for this reason that most convection ovens come with the option to turn the convection function on and off, depending on the needs of the particular dish.

HOT PLATE

A hot plate is a table- or countertop cooking appliance that substitutes for a built-in stovetop or cooktop. Usually consisting of one or two burners, most hot plates run on electricity, though it is possible to find gas powered versions, allowing for more portability.

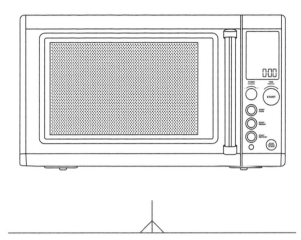

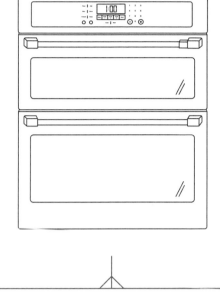

MICROWAVE OVEN

A microwave oven, often called a microwave for short, is a rectangular countertop appliance that cooks and heats food. A literal microwave, in the scientific sense, is an electromagnetic wave that is shorter than a radio wave but longer than an infrared wave. When applied to food, a microwave will agitate the water molecules contained within, producing friction and eventually heating your dish. Microwave ovens have existed since the mid-1960s, but didn't become common in American households for another decade or two. While there are certainly foods that do not fare well in microwave ovens, such as items that are meant to be crispy (see browning dish, page 68), other foods are now forever positively associated with microwave ovens—like popcorn.

OVEN

An oven is an appliance in which food is cooked in a heated, enclosed space. In most homes, the oven is powered by either a gas line or electricity, though originally, and still in many parts of the world, this cooking essential is fueled by burning wood, charcoal, or other substances. There are various types of ovens, but most simply an oven is just the lower portion of a range, and includes a dial or digital mechanism to adjust the heat level. Conventional ovens can have other functionalities, such as steaming or convection, or can be set to turn on and off at a particular time. In general, the world "oven" refers to any enclosed cooking space, as in a toaster oven or microwave oven.

RANGE/STOVE

A stove, also called a range, is a built-in appliance in the kitchen, which includes both a stovetop and an oven. In most developed countries, the stove is run with either gas (via an installed gas line) or is electric; however, stoves can also run on other burned fuel like wood or charcoal. Newer-fangled induction ranges and stoves work via an electromagnetic field, which transfers a current to magnetic-sensitive pots and pans, allowing them to heat up very quickly and efficiently.

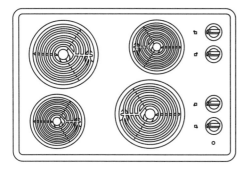

STOVETOP/COOKTOP

The stovetop, called a "hob" in the UK, is the horizontal portion of the stove that has burners upon which one situates pots and pans in order to cook food. Each burner has a knob that adjusts the level of heat, which is usually supplied via gas or electricity. Gas burners supply an adjustable flame, which is covered by a grate made of cast iron or other heat-safe material. Electric burners come in a variety of designs, from individual electric coils that balance pans, to glass- or ceramic-topped versions, that hide the electric element and provide a smooth surface on which to put cookware. Some modern stovetops offer induction burners, which operate by creating an electromagnetic field between the stovetop and the pan or pot, which in turn creates heat.

No-No's for Smooth Cooktops

Smooth surfaced electric cooktops, such as those made from glass or ceramic, are considered to be an aesthetic improvement over their coiled brethren, and visually this point is hard to argue. However, there is no question that the maintenance required for these beautified versions is more complicated. Be wary of spilling certain items on this cooktop, especially sugary substances, or letting a used spoon or greasy-bottomed pot sit on the cooktop, as the residual smears and splatters can burn and stain. Rougher types of cookware like cast iron, as well as heavy pots and pans, can also scratch the surface; even certain cleaners and sponges can be too abrasive and will cause lasting damage.

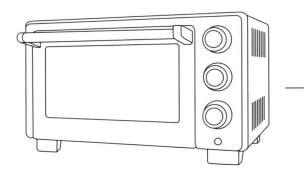

TOASTER OVEN

Unlike a slot toaster, in which bread is added vertically to a two-sided toasting mechanism, a toaster oven is a small countertop appliance that behaves more like a smaller version of a conventional oven. In this iteration, bread is toasted horizontally while lying flat on a built-in rack, with heating elements situated above and below. These two heating elements, in the form of coils, also give the toaster oven the ability to broil—by heating only the top coil and cooking an item from above—as well as to melt, which is a function of the appliance's horizontal cooking method. (Melting is a feat which cannot be achieved with a standard slot toaster, where the cheese or other substance would drip down into the mechanics of the machine.) Usually a toaster oven will come with a specially fitted tray to facilitate functions other than toasting, including small-batch baking and even roasting.

COOKWARE

Baking Dishes, Sheets & Tins

BAKING PAN

BAKING STONE/PIZZA STONE

BREAD PAN

BUNDT PAN/KUGELHOPF PAN

CASSEROLE

CLAY ROASTER/ROMERTOPF

COOKIE SHEET

CROCK

DOLSOT

HOTEL PAN

JELLY ROLL PAN

MUFFIN TIN

PIE PLATE

POPOVER PAN

ROASTING PAN

SHEET PAN

SOUFFLE DISH

SPRINGFORM PAN

These vessels are all used for baking or roasting, and come in a variety of shapes and sizes. Filled with batters, doughs, or individual ingredients, these metal or silicone containers sometimes work as a mold (page 101) as well as a cooking surface and conductor of heat, shaping the final product as it goes from raw to cooked.

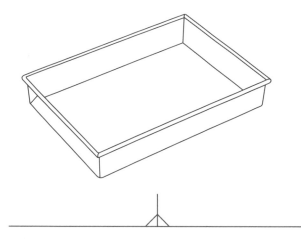

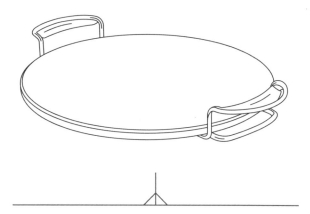

BAKING PAN

A commonly used vessel for making cakes, rolls, and roasted or baked meats and vegetables, the baking pan, also called a baking tray or cake pan, is a rectangular or round flat pan with medium high sides that are either vertical or slightly flared. Baking pans are often made of metal (stainless or nonstick), glass, or ceramic. Silicone versions are also popular, especially for cake making, as they're available in a wide array of shapes, including novelty forms like stars or hearts, and they're also naturally nonstick, which lessens the need for lining with parchment paper. Baking pans can be sold in sets, which is helpful when making layers of a multi-tiered cake that will eventually need to be stacked.

BAKING STONE/PIZZA STONE

A baking stone—and its popular subset, a pizza stone—is a heavy-duty surface one places in the oven, or on a grill. Once in place and preheated, raw breads, rolls, and other doughs are then positioned on the stone and allowed to cook. Usually made of clay or marble, this cooking surface is ideal for high-heat baking, like when making pizza, as its poor heat conduction means that the dough touching the surface of the stone will not burn before the rest of the food is cooked through. It is safest to place the stone in the oven prior to preheating, so it can come to temperature as slowly as possible; stones have been known to crack when burdened with sudden temperature changes. Pizza stones in particular are constructed using more porous materials that allow any extra moisture to be absorbed by the stone rather than the baking dough, resulting in a crispier crust.

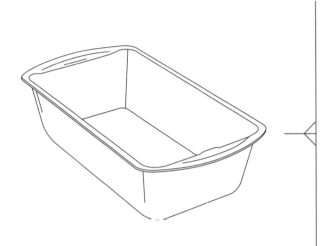

BREAD PAN

The bread pan, also known as a loaf pan, is a small- to medium-size rectangular pan with high sides that are vertical or slightly sloping. As its name suggests, the bread pan is most often used for baking bread. It is usually made out of metal, ceramic, or silicone, and sometimes has two ledges extending from the top of the short sides of the pan, acting as handles. The shape of the pan makes it conducive to baking other loaves, like meatloaf, or acting as a mold to set a layered food, like a terrine, ice box cake, or ice cream cake.

BUNDT PAN/KUGELHOPF PAN

A Bundt pan is a specialized metal, ceramic, or silicone pan that comes in a wide variety of designs, all of which add texture and three-dimensional interest to the outside of a cake while leaving a void in the center, resulting in a final product that is generally shaped like a ring. Some popular pans include fluting or ridges in their designs that add visual interest and make for easy portioning (just cut at the ridges). More uniquely shaped pans can be found in the form of a wreath, a rose, even a castle. Because of its esoteric surface, the Bundt pan requires special attention be paid prior to pouring any batter into the pan—even if it is a nonstick version of the pan, buttering and flouring every nook and cranny should be your first order of business.

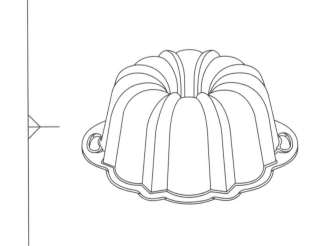

Minis

———○———

Per our biological predilection for small, cute things, most baking pans now have popular mini versions. Bundt pans, loaf pans, muffin tins, and more have been created in miniature, sometimes with multiple outlets in a single pan. Of course, one can use a recipe for a regular-size confection in these pans, but start checking for doneness significantly earlier, as these smaller baked goods will cook at a much faster rate.

CASSEROLE

A casserole dish, also called a baking dish, is a large pan with medium-high sides and two short handles that is used to cook food in the oven. Commonly made out of a ceramic material, other versions of a casserole dish have been made from glass, cast iron, or enameled carbon steel (similar to a Dutch oven). Typically, a casserole dish does not come with a lid, but often cooks will cover the dish with foil for a portion of the cooking time, as the dish's broad design means quick evaporation in the oven. Because of the saucy or layered nature of food one cooks in a casserole dish—think lasagna, enchiladas, baked chicken parts, and of course, casseroles—one often serves the dish directly from the cookware as well. A casserole dish can also be used in a bain-marie (page 87), as in the case of making a large flan.

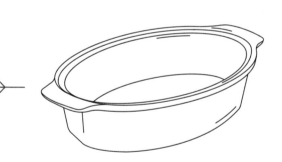

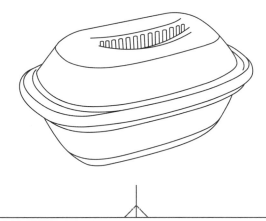

CLAY ROASTER/ROMERTOPF

A clay roaster, also called a Romertopf (from the German, meaning Roman pot) or terra-cotta roaster, is an unglazed ceramic vessel used for roasting food in the oven. Because of the porous and delicate nature of the unglazed clay, the roaster must be fully submerged in water for at least thirty minutes before each use. After it has been soaked, and ingredients have been added, the roaster may then be set into a cold oven only, before being brought to temperature slowly, so as not to shock the clay with high heat, which could result in cracking. The prepared clay roaster, which is often used to cook "low and slow," can then be used to bake all sorts of foods, from a whole chicken to a loaf of bread, even a stew. The slow release of steam from the previously soaked clay renders food especially tender. The clay roaster can come in a few different sizes and forms, including small specialty roasters made exclusively for heads of garlic. All roasters are sold with a fitted lid. Pots like a Dutch oven (page 88) or a cocotte (page 86) can cook similar types of dishes, but unlike those pots, the clay roaster cannot be used on a stovetop, so it provides less versatility in terms of browning meats prior to baking, or reducing a sauce before serving.

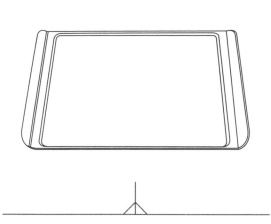

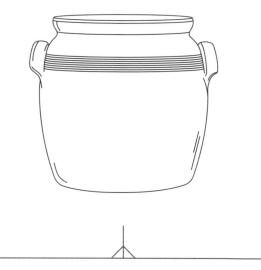

COOKIE SHEET

A cookie sheet is a flat, rectangular, thin metal pan used for baking and roasting in the oven. Per its name, this pan is especially adept at baking cookies, as its lack of rim makes it easy to slide the finished specimens onto a cooling rack (page 120). Some versions have one or two raised edges that function like handles. When fully rimmed (and more substantial in weight), a cookie sheet is no longer a cookie sheet, it's a sheet pan (page 64).

CROCK

A crock is an earthenware pot or jar that ranges in size. When used for cooking, large crocks are placed in the oven with a fitted lid. This style of pot is best used for stews, beans, and other items that require low-and-slow cooking, comparable to the modern Crock-Pot, an electric appliance that cooks similarly (see slow cooker, page 19). The thickness of a crock makes it oven safe and ideal for keeping its contents hot. Small crocks are good for melting cheese on top of individual servings of a French onion soup. Some lidded crocks are also used for preserving foods at room temperature, like sauerkraut or kimchi (which is traditionally buried underground to ferment). These versions have specialized lids that allow carbon dioxide to escape, causing the distinct flavors associated with fermentation.

DOLSOT

A *dolsot* is a very heavy, medium-size Korean bowl that is made out of stone and can be used for cooking on the stovetop or in the oven. The thickness of the dolsot's walls helps it retain heat very well and allows the vessel to continue cooking its contents long after it has been removed from a heat source. This is convenient as many traditional dishes are cooked in the dolsot and then served or eaten directly from it. Wonderful for cooking all sorts of soups, stews, and rice, a dolsot is a must for making and serving *dolsot bibimbap*, one of Korea's most famous dishes, that consists of short grain rice topped with a variety of prepared vegetables, pickles, meat, and an egg. Though most of these ingredients are added to the dolsot already cooked, the dolsot has the very important job of crisping the rice, which happens when the grain comes into direct contact with the bottom of the pot, creating a crust that adds an important texture to the finished dish.

HOTEL PAN

Hotel pans are rectangular metal vessels used by commercial and restaurant kitchens for prepping, cooking, and serving food. Their usage is very flexible as they are able to cook on a flattop, a stove, or in the oven, and they are often the pan of choice when serving from a steam table. In commercial kitchens, hotel pans are often used to by line chefs to hold prepared foods until they're needed to cook with. This versatile pan may also be used for presenting a variety of foods to customers in a commercial setting, such as in a salad bar or restaurant buffet. They come in a variety of standardized sizes, including a range of depths, and are sometimes paired with a fitted flat lid.

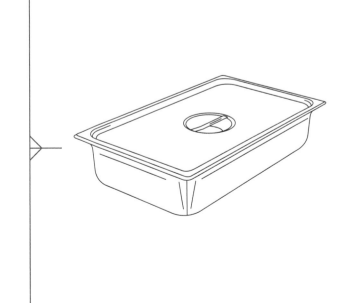

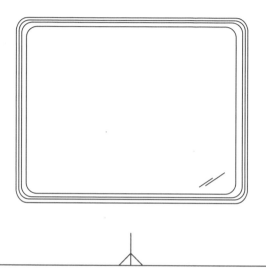

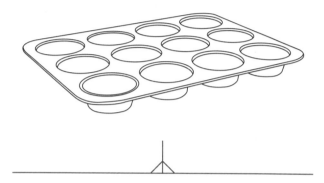

JELLY ROLL PAN

Despite its slightly more diminutive size, the jelly roll pan is almost identical to a sheet pan. It's a broad, flat, rectangular metal pan with four short vertical sides. It is called a jelly roll pan as it is intended for making a specific type of filled sponge cake called a jelly or Swiss roll, where the thin sheet of cake is spread with whipped cream, jam, curd, or custard, then rolled up and sliced crosswise into spiral-shaped servings. In addition to its use in making this specific cake, the jelly roll pan can be used for roasting, baking, and broiling. Likewise, one can make a jelly roll using a regular rimmed sheet pan.

MUFFIN TIN

A muffin tin is a metal or silicone pan with multiple molded concave indentations for baking cupcakes or muffins. In a standard muffin tin, the shape of the indentations is flat bottomed, with sloping sides, and the size of the indentations is consistent throughout the pan to allow for even cooking; however, tins can also come in jumbo, muffin top, and mini muffin sizes. Nonstick and silicone versions may not require paper cupcake liners (page 68) to hold the batter in the molds, but liners will be very helpful when using the standard metal type of tin as they will keep batter from sticking to the pan when baking.

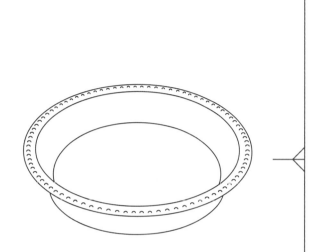

PIE PLATE

A pie plate is an oven-safe glass, metal, or ceramic dish meant for baking a pie. With a broad flat bottom and sloping sides, a pie plate is the only vessel available for making a standard circular pie. (Alternatively, one can make a slab pie in a rectangular baking sheet or pan, or a crostata, which doesn't have raised sides.) The sides or edge of the plate is sometimes decorated with fluting or simulated crimping to give the finished crust some dimension. Pie plates made from glass are arguably the best choice, for two reasons: first, one can see the color of the crust through the transparent glass, so you can be sure it is browned; and second, glass allows radiant heat to pass through it, which helps the crust get fully cooked and crisp. Since one both bakes and serves pie out of the same pan, tin disposable versions are popular when giving a pie as a gift, so one is not also gifting their pan.

Alternative Uses for Muffin Tins

In addition to making muffins, muffin tins can be used for cupcakes, rolls, Yorkshire Pudding, and even popovers, which are usually made in a taller specialized pan. A muffin tin can also make great individual quiches, frittatas, baked eggs, and meatloaf.

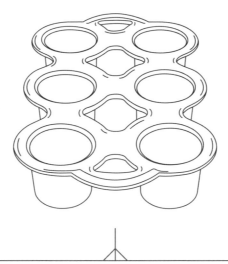

POPOVER PAN

This special, single-use pan was created to make a type of eggy, muffin-shaped quick bread known as a popover. Often confused with a muffin tin, a metal popover pan has a few unique design elements that set it apart and make it especially well-suited for popovers. Consisting of a set of concave cups that are filled with batter, the popover pan, as opposed to a muffin tin, is not constructed of a single, flat metal plane from which cups protrude (unless it has holes or gaps in the plane). In most cases, the cups are connected via a wire rack. The purpose of this design element is to promote better heat distribution and circulation around each cup, as popovers are extremely heat sensitive and require a blast of high heat to propel their structure up and out, "popping over" the top of the cups. Additionally, the depth of the individual cups is deeper than a traditional muffin tin, with steeper, almost vertical sides; this too helps to force the batter up, creating the popover's signature light, airy interior, as well as the browned, crispy exterior. Though some popover pans come with nonstick finishes, it is still imperative to generously grease the inside of the cups as the batter has a tendency to stick. While one could use a muffin tin to make popovers in a pinch, they will never be as puffy or as tall as when using a dedicated popover pan.

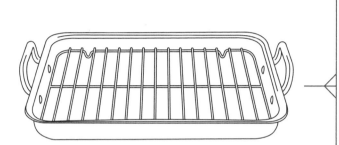

ROASTING PAN

A roasting pan is a broad rectangular pan that is most often used in the oven. With medium high sides and two short loop handles, this versatile pan is typically made of stainless steel and is adept at roasting, as well as baking and broiling. The bottom of the pan sometimes has grooved channels radiating away from the center, which drains liquid to the sides of the pan to help the food brown. Because it can function on the stovetop as well, one can deglaze a roasting pan and make a "pan sauce" on the stovetop after roasting in the oven has been completed. In some cases, such as with a turkey roasting pan, or turkey roaster, a lid and a fitted rack is included.

Popovers vs. Yorkshire Pudding

Popovers are made from a simple batter of flour, eggs, milk, and salt, and do not contain any leavening agents; the puff comes from the steam trapped inside the batter. Yorkshire Pudding—a traditional English side dish served with Sunday roast—is made of the same batter; however, there are two main differences that distinguish a popover from Yorkshire Pudding. First, Yorkshire Pudding's ultimate shape is more flexible—it can be poured into the individual cups of a popover pan, or all the batter can be poured into a ceramic dish or a large baking pan and shared. Second, the pan used to make popovers is usually greased with butter or oil, whereas Yorkshire Pudding uses beef drippings to grease the baking vessel. Traditionally, the batter for a Yorkshire Pudding was poured directly into the roasting pan where meat had been cooked.

SHEET PAN

A sheet pan—also called a rimmed baking sheet—is a broad, flat, rectangular, heavy-duty metal pan with a short, raised rim on all four sides. It is a multipurpose pan, great for baking thin cakes (similar to a jelly roll pan) and cookies, and broiling or roasting vegetables or meats. Because of its large size, it's also a helpful pan to use underneath casserole dishes with contents that might overflow into the oven. Half sheet pans (18 x 13 inches) are arguably the most common type of sheet pan found in home kitchens, as they fit easily into most standard ovens; full sheet pans are found in commercial kitchens, while quarter sheet pans are helpful for smaller jobs.

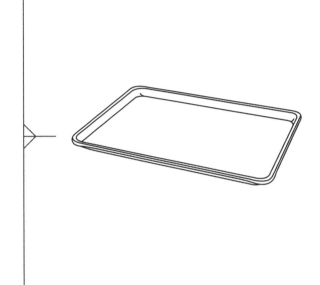

Preventing Sticking

When using any of the pans in this section, a cook often needs to consider the possibility of food sticking to the pan. Because batters and doughs are inherently wet, the chance of sticking is high, and one does not want to resort to cutting or scraping food away from the pan as the final shape of a baked good could be damaged. There are a few ways to prevent this from occurring when you're cooking. One option is to grease the pan with butter, oil, or cooking spray. If you're baking, coating the grease with a layer of crumbs or flour will provide further insurance, and especially in the case of an unusual or irregularly shaped pan like a Bundt pan, this two-step process is your best bet. Another option for straight sided or flat pans is to use parchment paper or foil to line the bottom and/or sides (if you use two crisscrossing pieces that overhang the sides, it can also be used as handles to help remove the final item from the pan). Muffin tins are best used with individual paper liners. When using any of these pans as molds, and not applying heat, plastic wrap can also be used to line the pan; this is a good option for ice cream cakes or terrines.

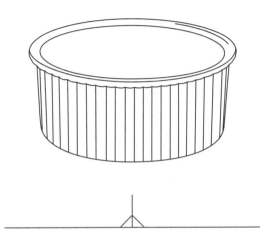

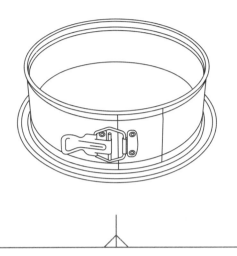

SOUFFLÉ DISH

A souffle dish is a round porcelain dish with tall vertical sides, similar in looks to a large ramekin (page 132). The sides of a soufflé dish are always straight and traditionally have a fluted design on the outside. Not surprisingly, this dish is most often used to make soufflés, a French egg dish that puffs up as it cooks, climbing up the sides of the ramekin until it creates a large bronzed cap on top. More versatile than it first appears, this dish is also good for cooking pot pies and other saucy or soupy recipes that include a topping of baked cheese or pastry.

SPRINGFORM PAN

A springform pan is a specialized round baking pan with vertical sides. The bottom of the pan is completely detached from the sides; a spring-loaded latch on the side walls cinches it into a circle, holding the bottom in place when baking. When the baking is finished, the latch can be undone so the sides release away from the cake and the bottom piece of the pan. The bottom piece can then be removed from the cake if necessary. This type of pan is very popular for making cheesccakes, as the spring release helps get the finished cake out of the pan without inverting it as one does regularly with other pans and other cakes. (Inverting the pan would cause damage to the cheesecake.) This is also a good pan for desserts with delicate crusts and frozen components, as they need to be handled less. While the bottom and sides of the pan usually nestle together well due to a fitted groove in the bottom piece, lining the pan with foil when adding a liquid batter is common practice to prevent any leaking.

Inserts & Lids

All of the pieces of cookware in this section are additions to pots, pans, and casseroles. They range from things made to be inserted into a pot or pan, like a rack or steamer, or things that rest on top, like a splatter screen or lid, all of which add value and functionality to the original vessel.

BAMBOO STEAMER

A bamboo steamer is a round lidded basket made of woven strips of bamboo. It is placed above simmering water in a pot or pan; food to be steamed is placed inside the basket and covered with the lid. As it evaporates, the steam from the simmering water flows through the porous weave of the steamer, gently cooking whatever is inside. The simplest versions of a bamboo steamer have one interior layer, but, especially in restaurant kitchens, multiple baskets can be stacked and covered with a single lid, creating different levels for different dishes. The steamers can be brought to the table for serving. Derived from Japanese and Chinese cultures, bamboo steamers are most often used to steam dumplings, egg dishes, fish, and vegetables.

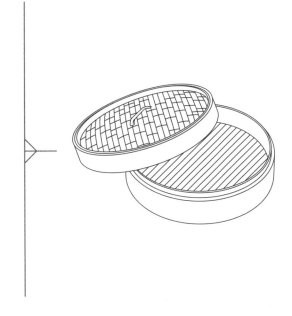

BROWNING DISH

Microwaves (page 47) are known for their inability to brown or caramelize foods; to amend this problem, browning dishes (also sometimes known as browning plates) were invented. A relatively obscure piece of equipment (perhaps due to the lessening appeal of microwave cooking), a browning dish, often manufactured by Corning Ware, works by preheating the dish in the microwave, then placing the food to be browned in it, covering with the specialized lid, and continuing to microwave.

CUPCAKE LINER/MUFFIN LINER

Because a cupcake pan has so much surface area, making it especially arduous to butter prior to adding batter, cupcake liners, which are dropped into each cupcake pan indentation and filled with batter, are a very convenient product that keeps cupcakes and muffins from sticking to the pan. Made of paper or foil, cupcake liners have a flat bottom and fluted sides which accordion in or out to fit any standard cupcake pan. Liners come in a variety of colors and patterns, since they are kept on the finished baked good until ready to eat.

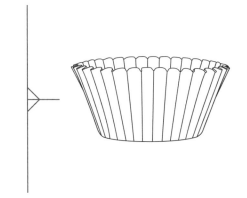

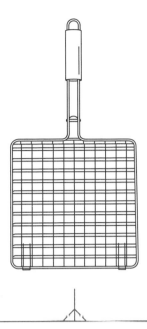

GRILL BASKET

A helpful piece of equipment employed when using an outdoor gas or charcoal grill, a grill basket is a vessel made of perforated metal, mesh, or woven wire that holds food as it is grilled. Typically, one would use a grill basket when the ingredients being cooked are small and/or include multiple pieces. In these cases, enclosing the food in a grill basket instead of laying it directly onto the grates of the grill keeps food from falling through the grates, while still exposing the food to the char and smoke of the fire. A grill basket is also helpful for grilling delicate foods that might stick to the grates of the grill or tear when you try to flip them, like fish. When using a grill basket, one is able to flip the entire basket over to grill the opposite side, all while the food is nestled safely inside. There are a variety of styles of grill basket. Some versions are enclosed flat cages, which suspend food between two hinged sides that latch together; this option saves time and trouble, as it allows the person

doing the grilling to flip a slew of ingredients all at once. This style is best suited for grilling fish or slices of vegetables, like eggplant or zucchini. Another, open-air style (sometimes called a grilling tray), features a flat metal sheet with no closeable top. This version can come with or without raised sides but include perforations or slits that are not large enough to drop and lose ingredients, and allow the heat and smoke through the holes. This style of grill basket can cook recipes that include many small pieces, like cut up potatoes, cherry tomatoes, or shrimp; depending on the density of the mesh or perforations, one can stir and flip the food in these just as you would a regular pan. (Alternatively, in these cases, one can use a skewer, page 267, instead of a grill basket to keep foods from falling through the grill's grates.) Any of these grill baskets can also be used without a grill or grill grates by propping the baskets directly over a live fire or embers.

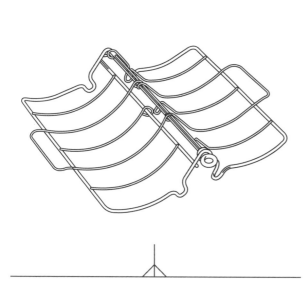

ROASTING RACK

A roasting rack is a freestanding metal rack that sits atop or inside a larger roasting pan or baking sheet, and is used to raise items being cooked so that they are not sitting on the bottom of the pan. This allows the hot air of the oven to circulate around the ingredients, cooking and browning them evenly. For example, many oven-fried chicken recipes recommend employing a roasting rack to ensure that the entire exterior of each piece of chicken gets crispy. The roasting rack also drains away fat from the food as it cooks, as is the case with cooking bacon in the oven. Often coated in silicone for easier cleanup, roasting racks come in a variety of shapes ranging from flat, to U- or V-shaped. Some versions also have adjustable sides that you can customize to ensure they fit all oven sizes and your ingredients. A roasting rack with sides is usually used for roasting poultry.

ROTISSERIE

A rotisserie is a cooking accessory or appliance consisting of a rotating spit that spins foods on an axle as it cooks. Most rotisseries either come with their own specialized heating elements, or they are meant to be combined with another cooking source, like a grill. The spit may be designed to include baskets or extra prongs for stability, and can be turned manually or, in some instances, via a small motor. A rotisserie is meant to counteract the problems of using a cooking source that emits heat from only one direction and is not enclosed enough to contain the heat, like a fire, or an open grill. By spinning the food, one is able to use the same source and have the food cook evenly.

Dinner on a String

The rotisserie (opposite page)—a device made to continuously turn a roast or whole bird in front of a heating element—is a wonderful way to cook large pieces of meat. But prior to the invention of rotisseries, more primitive solutions abounded. Enter a method of cooking using only string (see kitchen twine, page 116) and a live fire: sometimes called string roasting. In this method, one trusses the piece of meat, leaving an extra length of string attached, and hangs it from a height, so that it dangles close enough to the fire to cook slowly and steadily. Hanging it from the mantelpiece in front of a fireplace is an option, as is setting up a similar dynamic around a campfire. In both cases, placing a drip pan below the meat is a necessity and will capture flavorful juices. To prevent only the fire-facing side of the roast from cooking, the meat is gently spun on the string, which will uncoil and recoil itself repeatedly, spinning to present all sides of the meat to the fire for even cooking. Besides spinning the meat once in a while, the only other action needed is kindling the fire well enough to cook the meat through: a low maintenance method with high impact results.

SILICONE LID

Heat-safe silicone makes for a versatile and convenient universal lid for pots and pans. Sometimes plain, sometimes punctured with vents, a silicone lid is a helpful addition when you want to keep the moisture in a cooking vessel, but your cookware does not have its own designated lid. For example, when using a steamer basket (page 73) placed inside a saucepot, one might top the pot with a silicone lid so the items inside steam evenly. As an added bonus, silicone doesn't conduct heat well, which makes it easier to handle.

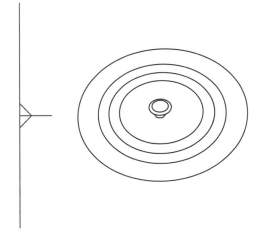

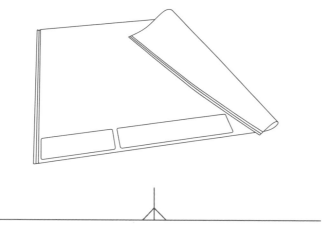

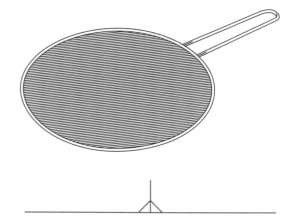

SILICONE MAT

Instead of lining your baking or cookie sheet with disposable parchment or foil, consider a reusable option: a silicone mat. A thick padded sheet that can be washed by hand or in the top rack of a dishwasher, a silicone mat provides a nonstick surface for both prep and cooking. By placing a silicone mat on a cookie or baking sheet and putting on the bottom rack of the oven, the mat protects your oven and bakeware from casserole dishes or pie plates that threaten to bubble over on the top rack. A mat can also serve as a cooking surface by placing cookie dough or meringues directly atop the mat to bake. By adding an extra layer between the pan and the dough, a silicone mat allows for less heat conductivity and ensures that the bottom of cookies and other baked items will not brown at a faster rate than the rest of the dough. On its own, a silicone mat is especially well suited as a work surface for candy making; for example, melted chocolate or brittle can be poured onto the mat, put in the freezer to chill, and then peeled off easily when solidified.

SPLATTER SCREEN

A circular sheet of mesh with a long wire handle, a splatter screen is a tool that sits atop a pan and functions like a lid, creating a physical barrier meant to prevent the splattering of the pan's contents while still allowing steam to escape. Often used for deep or shallow frying, a splatter screen prevents grease or other hot bubbling liquids from sputtering out of the pan and onto your cooktop or hands. It might be tempting to use a lid as a makeshift splatter screen, but this is not a true alternative since the steam and condensation forming inside the pot are not able to escape through a solid lid; this will also cause the temperature inside the pan to rise, affecting the cooking time of the contents.

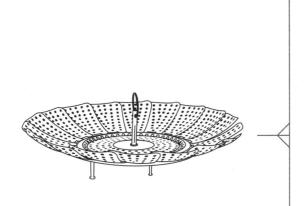

STEAMER BASKET

A steamer basket is necessary for most types of steaming, a technique that uses gentle but very hot vapor to cook food. Generally, a steamer basket is made of perforated, loosely woven, or vented stainless steel or silicone that can be fixed in shape or collapsible, allowing them to be adjusted to fit different-size cooking vessels. Wooden or bamboo versions are available as well, such as the bamboo steamer (page 68). Placed in a pot or pan above boiling water, the loose frame of a steamer basket allows hot air to circulate around the food placed inside; a lid is highly recommended as it helps contain the steam for faster cooking.

Steaming Tactics

Depending on the type of food being steamed, there are multiple ways to use a steamer. In many cases, food can be placed directly on the surface of a bamboo, silicone, or metal steamer to cook, though some sticking may occur if the surface of the food gets tacky as it cooks, like in the case of dumplings or fish. In these cases, line the steamer with a lettuce or cabbage leaf, then lay down the delicate food on top; these leaves also make for easy (and compostable) clean up. If the ingredient is liquid (like eggs or custard), or steamed with a sauce or other accoutrement, consider placing it in a small bowl, cup, or plate before placing in the steamer. It is also recommended to use a container within the steamer if the juices released during cooking will be a complementary part of the dish.

Pans

As opposed to pots, whose depth makes them ideal for cooking with liquids, pans are flatter than they are tall (for the most part), which makes them especially adept at searing and sautéing as they allow liquid to evaporate more easily.

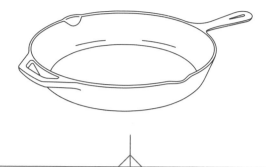

CAST-IRON SKILLET

Considered one of the most versatile pans, a cast-iron skillet is a flat-bottomed pan with a short handle that is able to sauté, fry, bake, roast, and more. The pan's iron core, which is casted into various shapes and sizes (and sometimes coated in enamel or ceramic), holds heat incredibly well, making it an especially excellent choice for searing, as the temperature of the pan will barely drop when ingredients are added, even if they are cold or room temperature. In addition to the stovetop, oven, and broiler, a cast iron skillet also fares well on an open fire; some types of cast-iron skillets even include legs that will allow the skillet to balance over a charcoal or wood fire. The "seasoning" on a cast-iron pan—the thin layers of grease on the cooking surface that harden into a makeshift nonstick surface—is best achieved by years of careful use and gentle cleaning. Because they are so durable, a well-seasoned pan is prized, and often handed down from one generation to the next. One note of caution: Beware of cooking acidic foods, like tomatoes, in cast iron, as they will react to the iron content and can give your food a metallic taste.

Caring for Your Cast Iron

How to clean a cast-iron pan, or how not to, is the root of many an argument. But here are a few undeniable facts: soap is not good for the seasoning of the pan, and cleaning immediately and drying thoroughly prevent it from getting rusty. Ideally, swipe with a non-soapy sponge or scrubber and rinse in warm water to clean, then put it on a low flame on the stove for a few minutes to evaporate every bit of moisture. Then be sure to season the pan as often as necessary to maintain its smooth finish.

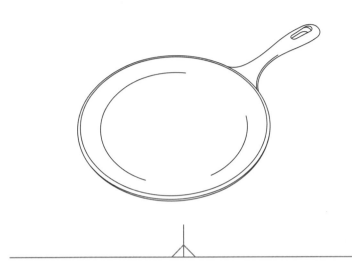

COMAL

The comal is a heavy, circular, flat pan with a small handle and a short, raised ridge around the edge. Usually made of noncoated cast iron, other less-common versions of the comal can be oblong or rectangular in shape, allowing the pan to straddle two burners. In addition, slightly concave versions made of clay were popular prior to the existence of cast iron and are still seen occasionally. A cross between a cast-iron skillet and a griddle, this traditional pan is indigenous to Mexico and Central and South America and is used primarily to cook tortillas. Often dated to pre-Columbian times, the traditional comal is very versatile and can be used to sear meats, toast seeds and nuts, and roast vegetables, among other tasks. Like all other cast-iron cookware, this pan can be used in the oven as well as on the stovetop or on the grill, and it retains heat exceptionally well. However, just like a cast-iron skillet, a cast-iron comal does need to be seasoned and treated carefully to keep its surface smooth and free of rust, and it should not be exposed to soap or be allowed to soak (see Caring for Your Cast Iron, opposite page).

EGG POACHING PAN

An egg poaching pan is a less common piece of kitchen equipment, created for the single use of poaching multiple eggs at once. The base of the pan is shaped like a sauté pan, with a broad bottom, short vertical sides, and a lid, but the pan is also sold with a set of specialized cups that sit inside the pan. To use, one fills the cavity of the pan with simmering water, cracks a single egg into each cup, then covers the pan and cooks until the eggs are done. While a bit of a misnomer, as poaching means cooking something directly in a simmering liquid, the egg poaching pan could be a convenience for a home cook whose favorite egg preparation could use streamlining.

EGG SPOON

The esoteric and rare egg spoon is a tool made exclusively for one purpose: frying a single egg. Made of metal—in fact, often hand-forged out of iron—this weighty spoon is part utensil and part pan, and has an extra-long handle and a small but deep concave bowl just large enough to hold a single egg out of its shell. The long handle, which can make the spoon around 16 inches in total length, is meant to facilitate the cooking of the egg over a wood fire. This method of egg frying means the final product will absorb some of the flavor from the smoke of the fire. Reportedly, the proximity to the heat source and the hands-on nature of the spoon itself gives cooks a special affinity for the egg spoon and the food it creates, despite the large amount of resources required (wood and fuel, the time taken to burn down to embers, etc.), at least relative to simply frying an egg in a pan on a stovetop. A specialized tool for sure, the popularity of the egg spoon increased greatly when Alice Waters made known her personal affection for it, and used it to cook Lesley Stahl an egg on *60 Minutes*.

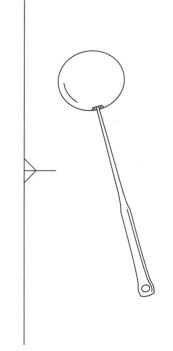

GRILL PAN

Created to mimic the type of cooking one does on an outdoor barbeque, the grill pan is a broad, square or round pan with a long handle that has distinctly raised ridges running across its cooking surface. This pan also comes in an extra-large rectangular shape that fits across two burners on the stove, often with a flat griddle on one side and a ridged grill pan on the other. Like the grates of a standard outdoor grill, the ridges of a grill pan raise food above the flat surface of the pan, creating a grill's signature blackened stripes on the food. These ridges also drain fat and juices away from the food as it cooks, which is why grilling is considered a somewhat lean cooking style, as there's no added fat to cook the food in. While the grill pan is able to cook food in a style similar to that of an outdoor grill, the grill pan cannot provide any of the added smoke flavor or flame-kissed char that comes from using the real thing.

RONDEAU/BRAZIER

A rondeau, also called a brazier or braiser, is a type of broad shallow pot with two loop handles and a slightly domed, tight fitting lid. Shallower than a Dutch oven and wider than a sauce pot, this heavy-duty pot is usually made of coated cast iron or stainless steel, and can conduct heat very well. The rondeau can be used to cook on top of the stove as well as in the oven, making it the ideal vessel for braised dishes. Additionally, the relatively short height of the sides of the pot means one can easily brown meat or vegetables prior to adding liquid and placing in the oven, and then quickly reduce a sauce after cooking.

Vocabulary Lesson

The words *saucepot* and *saucepan* are often used interchangeably, but the products these words refer to are actually quite different. Somewhat less popular than its counterpart, a saucepot (page 91) is a smaller version of a stockpot, featuring two short handles and a lid, and often made in stainless steel or ceramic-coated cast iron. A saucepot is good for stewing and braising, or cooking rice. A saucepan (page 80), with its single long handle and taller frame, is better for boiling and blanching, as one can easily use the long handle to turn the contents out into a colander (page 217).

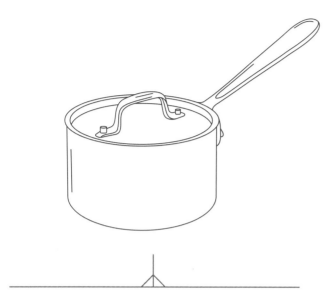

SAUCEPAN

A saucepan is a deep, straight-sided pan that is often as tall as it is wide. Made with a medium-narrow bottom, a long handle, and a corresponding lid, the depth of the saucepan and the length of its handle make it a good pan for boiling and blanching. As such, this pan is often used for cooking pasta, vegetables, beans, and oatmeal. A must-have in any home kitchen, the versatility of the saucepan, especially one made of heavy-duty stainless steel or copper, is unparalleled.

SAUCIER

A saucier is a medium-size pan with a rounded bottom and tall sloping sides that is traditionally made of either stainless steel, copper, or aluminum. This particular pan's design makes it best for using with liquids and loose-textured foods like sauces (hence the name of the pan, which when roughly translated from the French means a cook who specializes in making sauce), custards, and risottos. Since there is no hard-angled bottom perimeter for ingredients to get stuck on (unlike a sauté pan, for example), the saucier allows a cook to easily and thoroughly stir or whisk whatever contents it contains. A saucier is often paired with a corresponding lid, and sometimes has a small loop handle in addition to its long handle, which is helpful when moving a full saucier of liquid, which can be quite heavy.

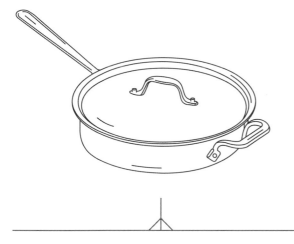

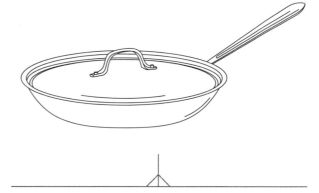

SAUTÉ PAN

A broad, flat-bottomed pan with short, straight sides, the sauté pan is often packaged with a corresponding lid, and typically has a long handle as well as a small opposing loop handle. These design elements and the pan's overall shape make it a superior option for shallow frying or braising, as the sauté pan can hold more volume than a correspondingly large skillet, and also offers a larger amount of flat cooking surface. A sauté pan is also a good option for searing, roasting and . . . sautéing. Most commonly, sauté pans are made of uncoated stainless steel, but nonstick and ceramic-coated versions abound, as well versions made of cast iron, aluminum, and copper.

SKILLET/FRYING PAN

A skillet, or frying pan, is a flat-bottomed pan with a long handle and short slanting sides that comes in a variety of sizes. One of the most common and well-used pans in a kitchen, most skillets are able to be used on top of the stove as well as in the oven; they can also sear, sauté, roast, bake, and more. Most commonly made of stainless steel, some skillets are made of cast iron (as previously noted), aluminum, or even copper. A number of skillets also come with ceramic or nonstick coating. Nonstick skillets can be very convenient, but the special surface should not be used for broiling or high temperature baking—consult the manufacturer for specifics.

What Pan to Use When

Confusingly, the names of some pans do not necessarily coordinate with their best use. With its sloping sides, a skillet or frying pan is really best used for sautéing, not frying, as the pan allows a cook to easily toss ingredients single handedly without using a utensil. On the other hand, a sauté pan is really best used for shallow frying, as the hot oil is more easily contained by the vertical sides of the pan, reducing the possibility of oil sloshing out of the pan and onto the cook. Note too that purchasing the same size of pan—say 10 inches—in both a sauté pan and a skillet/frying pan option will result in two pans with very different cooking surface areas. A pan's diameter is measured from the top of its sides, not the bottom. Since a sauté pan has vertical sides that go straight up and down, if you buy a 10-inch pan, you will have roughly 10 inches across of cooking surface. A skillet/frying pan has sloping sides, and buying a 10-inch pan will actually result in a much smaller amount of cooking surface, likely closer to 7 or 8 inches across.

SPLAYED SAUTÉ PAN

A more obscure pan, the splayed sauté pan has a flat bottom and tall sloping sides, making it a cross between a shorter-sided skillet and a rounder saucier (page 80). This pan is best for recipes where both browning and braising will occur, like a stew, as the splayed sauté pan can accommodate a lot of liquid in addition to offering the surface area needed for searing. This pan is most typically found in stainless steel or copper.

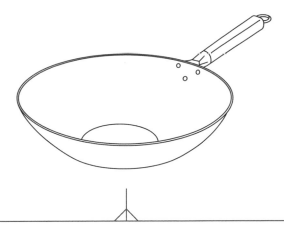

WOK

A thin-walled hemispherical pan with high, rounded sides and a small tapered bottom, a wok is a traditional and incredibly common piece of cooking equipment in much of Asia—especially in China, where the wok originated around 3,000 years ago. Usually made of seasoned carbon steel, cast iron, stainless steel, aluminum, or copper (nonstick versions are discouraged as they cannot sear well), woks come in a wide variety of sizes, and are usually packaged with a lid and, occasionally, a rack for steaming. Round bottomed versions are traditional, but flat-bottomed options are more common in Western kitchens, since a flat-bottomed pan is able to sit firmly on a Western-style cooktop (page 48). Versatile and light for its size, a wok is adept at most stovetop cooking techniques: sautéing, deep-frying, searing, stewing, and boiling, among others. In spite of its myriad uses, a wok is most widely known and used for its stir-frying capabilities. Stir-frying is the singular technique of cooking food quickly in a small amount of oil. The wok's special design both concentrates heat around its small bottom and allows the heat to dissipate in intensity as it moves up the rounded sides of the pan and away from the heat source. This allows a cook to move food to different parts of the pan in order to speed up or slow its cooking.

Wok Hay

Wok hay, roughly translated as the "breath of a wok," is the exalted essence of wok cooking. Wok hay is usually attributed to the masterful sear and char one is able to achieve by stir-frying in a well-seasoned and properly heated wok; it is a prized quality that is not achieved easily. If one crowds the pan or tries to stir-fry wet ingredients, one will never achieve wok hay.

Pots

Pots—cooking vessels with two handles, usually tall enough to hold a large amount of liquid—are a fundamental tool for making stocks, soups, and stews. Often paired with a lid, pots are usually made of metal and can be used on the stovetop as well as in the oven. It's helpful to have at least a couple of pots in different sizes in a kitchen.

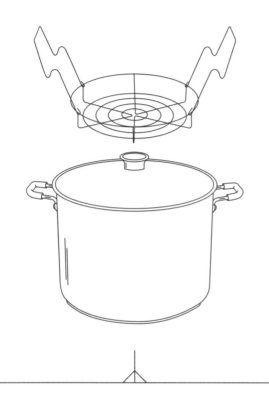

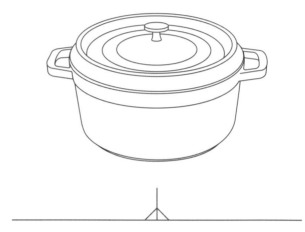

CANNING POT

A canning pot is used for processing canning jars (page 99) by boiling them for a specified amount of time. Formally, canning pots are just large lidded pots, tall enough to cover the jars by at least a few inches of water. A large stock pot (page 91) can easily substitute. Specific canning pots are packaged with a removable metal rack, as the jars must not touch the bottom of the pot while being boiled; some rack designs can also be used to lift and lower the jars into the pot.

COCOTTE

Interchangeable with a Dutch oven, a cocotte is the French term for a heavy-duty ceramic casserole dish with high sides and a fitted lid. Usually cast in iron and then covered in ceramic, a cocotte is best used for low and slow cooking in the oven. (See Dutch oven, page 88, for more details.) Mini cocottes have become popular in recent years for baking individual servings of pasta or pot pies; they are also often used as salt cellars (page 104).

DOUBLE BOILER

A double boiler is actually two pots nestled together. One pot sits on top of the stove, and a second, slightly smaller pot is then fitted inside or on top of the first. The purpose of the double boiler is to create a gentle cooking environment for heating or reheating delicate foods. Common tasks associated with a double boiler include melting chocolate or whisking a hollandaise. The pot works by first boiling a few inches of water in the bottom chamber, then resting the top pot above without letting it touch the boiling water below. The steam from the boiling water will heat the surface of the top pot, allowing for a gentle cooking of whatever food is placed in it. If one does not own a double boiler, an easy substitution is a pot of shallow boiling water, with a heat-safe metal or glass bowl that rests snugly on the pot's rim.

Bain-Marie vs. Double Boiler

Like a double boiler, a water bath or bain-marie—translated from French, it means Marie's bath—is used to cook delicate foods, like custards and cheesecakes. The two are often mistaken for each other, though there are differences, starting with the fact that a double boiler is a piece of equipment, while the bain-marie is really more of a technique. A double boiler is used on the stovetop and relies on steam heat rising from below to cook the contents in the upper pot. A bain-marie refers to cooking something in a container that sits directly in a hot water bath, most often in the oven. Flan, for example, is cooked in a bain-marie: the custard is poured into a ceramic or glass dish that sits in a larger roasting pan; hot water is poured in the roasting pan until it reaches about halfway up the dish and the whole thing is then placed in the oven to cook. The bain-marie provides more even cooking for the custard and generates steam to keep it from drying out.

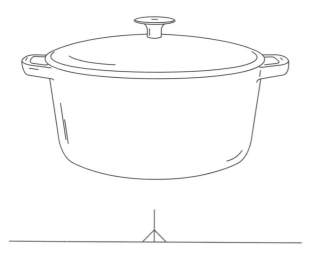

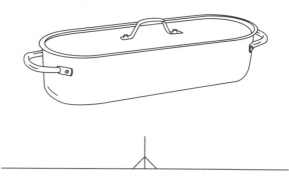

DUTCH OVEN

A Dutch oven is a very heavy cast-iron pot with a tight-fitting lid that can be used on the stovetop or in the oven. They are called Dutch because their creation in the seventeenth century in the UK was modeled on a Dutch technique for casting bronze, though the English used iron instead, as a cheaper alternative. The cast iron used in a Dutch oven is either seasoned or coated in enamel; either way it's a very efficient heat conductor. Dutch ovens come in a variety of sizes and shapes, and are very versatile, able to sauté, boil, bake, braise, fry, and more. Dutch ovens are also sturdy enough to be used on a campfire; in fact, some versions are designed specifically for this environment, with legs to hold the pot above coals, and an indented lid to hold additional coals on top, allowing heat to radiate into the Dutch oven from below and above.

FISH KETTLE

A fish kettle, also called a fish poacher, is a short oblong lidded pot, used specifically for cooking a whole fish on top of the stove. A bit old fashioned and certainly specialized, the fish kettle is the best cookware to poach or steam an entire fish or side of fish because of its oval shape; there are not many substitutions. However, one can cook the whole fish in an alternate pan in the oven, or cut the fish into a more manageable size to cook in another vessel.

FONDUE POT

Made of stoneware, enameled cast iron, porcelain, or ceramic, a fondue pot—also known as a *caquelon* in French—is a thick substantial pot with a short, stout handle that sits on a small tabletop burner, for traditional Swiss fondue. The heartiness of the pot retains the heat well, helping to keep the cheese melted, and the thickness of the bottom helps prevent the cheese from scorching while the fondue is being eaten. Sometimes a fondue pot is packaged with a set of fondue forks—long-handled, double pronged utensils best for spearing a piece of bread and dipping it into the fondue.

After the Fondue

When the majority of the fondue is gone, the thin layer of remaining cheese in a fondue pot will become toasted and crispy if allowed to sit over the burner. This treat on the bottom of the pot is called *"la religieuse,"* translated as "the nun," and is considered a delicacy to be shared among the diners.

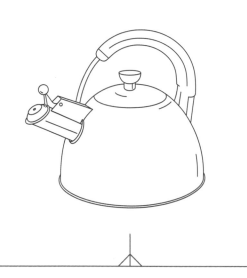

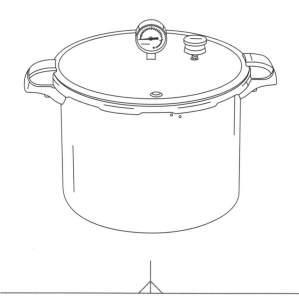

KETTLE

A kettle is an enclosed vessel for heating water. A bulbous container, lidded with a handle and spout, the kettle makes boiling water on top of the stove and serving it more efficient and easier than in a regular pot. Electric kettles plug into a wall outlet rather than using the stovetop, heat water very quickly, and are popular especially in tea-drinking cultures. Before indoor plumbing, extra-large kettles were used to heat water for cleaning and bathing as well.

PRESSURE CANNER

A pressure canner is an aluminum pot used for canning foods like meat and vegetables, whose lower acidic levels mean a higher temperature canning process is required to preserve them. This stovetop pot creates a controlled, pressurized environment, where the boiling point of water can be raised from the standard 211.19°F (99.97°C) to the 240°F (115.56°C) required to kill all harmful bacteria and safely preserve low acid foods. To use, the chosen ingredients are prepared and added to sterilized canning jars (page 99), then placed in the pressure canner with a nominal amount of water, and processed according to directions. In addition to a simple pot, the canner includes a locking lid with a pressure release valve and a pop-up pressure indicator, which lets you know that there is pressure building and, therefore, the canner is doing its job. High acid foods, like a pickle or acidic fruit, can be canned using a simpler, water bath method.

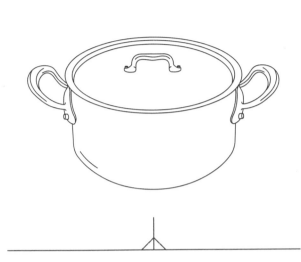

SAUCEPOT

The saucepot is a less common type of pot, often confused with its more celebrated relative, the saucepan, though in appearance it more closely resembles a small stockpot. (See Vocabulary Lesson, page 79, for more discussion on the differences between this pot and others.) The saucepot is a wide metal pot with medium-short, straight sides. Often made of stainless steel, many saucepots come with two loop handles and a tight-fitting lid. Per its name, the saucepot is the ideal piece of equipment for cooking dishes that include a sauce, as the large surface area on the bottom of the pot aids in evaporation. The saucepot is also great for braising, as its capacity is large and the wide surface area is good for any preliminary meat browning that may be required prior to adding liquid.

STOCK POT

A stock pot is an extra-large, extra-tall pot primarily used for making stocks, but also good for large volume boiling, like cooking lobsters, pasta, or ears of corn. Since this pot is so large and usually filled with liquid, the metal material it's made from is usually lighter than a regular pot, allowing for easier transport and cleaning in the kitchen.

KITCHEN ACCESSORIES

Containers, Holders & Molds

The kitchen is full of tools and equipment whose purpose is to hold or house foodstuffs. A simple mixing bowl is necessary for combining multiple items together. Some containers create special vacuum-sealed or humidity-free environments; others are shaped in a distinct way in order to mold the final product.

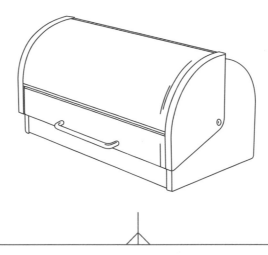

BREAD BOX

A bread box is a closed container designed to hold and keep bread and baked goods at room temperature. As opposed to storing one's bread in a plastic wrapper or a paper bag, the bread box creates an ideal environment for a loaf from a bakery, which has a crunchy crust and a soft interior. Typically situated on a kitchen countertop, the bread box keeps humidity out, and therefore prevents the loaf from molding, while still allowing just enough airflow to let the bread breathe, which keeps it from going stale. Store-bought bread, with its additives and preservatives, will not keep as well in a breadbox, as it is created specifically to stay in its own wrapper. This type of bread, it should be noted, does not have a crispy or crusty exterior to be maintained, so encasing it in plastic will not harm the texture. But bakery bread, which could otherwise go stale in less than twenty-four hours, is very at home in a bread box. The box itself can be made of metal (usually tin or stainless steel), wood, plastic, or ceramic. Each have their own benefits; wood is the most breathable, but others may be easier to clean and maintain. Bread box lids are often roll topped or hinged, though some plastic versions have a snap on lid that functions more simply—a bit like a vented Tupperware container.

Standard of Yesterday

Nowadays, in the US at least, most bread is prepackaged and purchased at the grocery store, and the bread itself contains chemical additives to help keep it fresh. Yet with present day concerns about preservatives and the appeal of artisan food, throwbacks like the humble bread box might be making a comeback. But even with a bump in popularity, the bread box is not nearly as prolific as it once was. Before packaged bread was common, most people bought their bread at a bakery and needed a way to keep it fresh for as long as possible. Thus, many households owned and used a bread box with great regularity. Keeping this in mind, is it any surprise that in the spoken game of deductive reasoning "20 Questions," a standard question is "Is it bigger than a bread box?". At one time, everyone playing would have understood and agreed to the size of a standard bread box. (This question was first posed on the game show *What's My Line?* in the 1950s, and took off in popularity, so much so that players at home asked it when playing themselves.) However, the real question these days is whether the same shared knowledge regarding the size of a bread box still exists, and whether it remains universal enough to give any modern-day players of "20 Questions" a true sense of scale.

CAKE TURNTABLE

A cake turntable, also known as a revolving cake stand, is used by professional pastry chefs (and enthusiastic home cooks) to make the process of decorating round cakes easier and faster. With a stable bottom that elevates the cake and a plate on top that is able to be spun, a cake turntable makes it easier to create a finished surface on a frosted or iced cake. To use, one centers a cake on the turntable, then applies frosting on the top and sides using a decorating comb (page 181), straight spatula, or offset spatula. Next, instead of maneuvering the frosting around using the spatula, one holds the utensil still against the side of the cake with one hand, and then spins the cake around with the other. This maneuver helps to make the frosting consistently thick. The spinning also makes it easier to apply other decorations—such as those made with a pastry bag (page 182) and tips (page 183)—to the cake, as the cake can turn instead of the decorator.

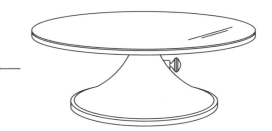

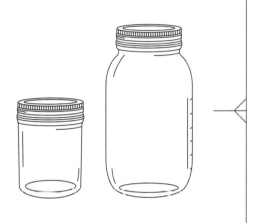

CANNING JARS

Canning jars are the containers used to process and hold homemade jams, jellies, chutneys, pickles, and other preserves. There are multiple parts to a canning jar: the glass jar, the metal lid with a rubber sealing edge, and the band that screws the lid onto the jar. Water bath and pressure canning both use canning jars, which come in a variety of sizes. The cooking of the filled jars to a high temperature kills contaminants and removes the air from the jar; the subsequent cooling of the hot jars creates a vacuum seal that prevents spoilage.

FUNNEL

A funnel is a kitchen tool used to facilitate transferring liquid foods and finely ground ingredients, like spices or dry goods, into a vessel or container. For instance, a funnel is often used for canning purposes, so that one can fill canning jars (above) without dirtying the rim of the jar. A funnel is essentially a vertical tube with a very wide top, which makes adding ingredients to the funnel easy and neat; the funnel then tapers down into a tube, creating a passage for the ingredients to pass through. The shape, size, and length of the neck, as well as the dimensions of a funnel vary greatly depending on the task one is planning to perform. Funnels comes in a variety of materials including plastic, aluminum, stainless steel, and glass, and some also include a built-in filter to strain the funneled items.

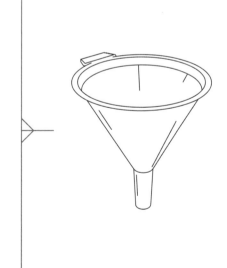

ICE CUBE TRAY

An ice cube tray is a mold that holds water or other liquids and is placed in the freezer until it is solid, creating ice. It comes in a variety of sizes and styles, with a varying number of compartments, including novelty shapes like large spheres for cocktails, which melt very slowly; or long ice sticks, for adding to a thin-necked water bottle. Metal ice cube trays were the norm in days past, but most modern trays are made from plastic or silicone. Depending on the tray's material and associated rigidity, one removes the ice cubes by cracking the tray with a simple twist, which releases the cubes from their compartments, or by flexing the silicone compartments to eject each individual piece.

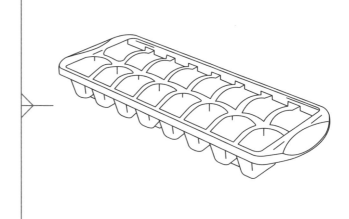

The Many Uses of Ice Cube Trays

In addition to freezing water, there are many uses for ice cube trays for the creative and waste-conscious cook. Some cooks use the trays to freeze small amounts of sauces (pesto, adobo, etc.) and stocks, then store the cubes in the freezer and add these small amounts to dishes for a punch of additional flavor. This technique can also be used to prevent discarding leftover dribs and drabs (like the remains of a can of broth), as they can be preserved and used in the future. Thinking ahead, the ice cube tray can be used to freeze other liquids, such as coffee, creating cubes that can be added to a drink to chill it without eventually watering it down—think iced coffee, with coffee ice cubes. The small size of the compartments also make it convenient for preserving small amounts of food. Parents can use ice cube trays to freeze a batch of vegetable puree and other baby foods; the eventual frozen cubes can be easily melted one by one for a single serving.

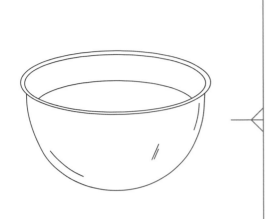

MIXING BOWL

A mixing bowl is made especially for combining ingredients together: larger and deeper than a serving bowl to prevent ingredients from spilling over the edges while being mixed, and durable enough to handle anything from a whisk to a handheld mixer working inside it. The mixing bowl is typically made from stainless steel, ceramic, glass, copper, or plastic, and often comes as part of a set of varying sizes, thereby increasing versatility and offering the ability to mix several sets of ingredients at once, as in when baking, for example.

MOLD

A mold is used to shape foods, as in the process of making terrines and pâtés, puddings and gelatins, cakes, ice cream, and more. To help hold the final shape, the food itself must go through a transformative process while in the mold—steaming, baking, chilling, and so on—so that by the time it is removed from the mold, it will have gained enough structure to maintain its new shape; an example would be a mousse that is poured into an individual mold and refrigerated. After chilling, the mousse will be set enough to be removed from the mold, garnished, and served. Historically, molds are made from metal, ceramic, plastic, or glass, and require preparation (like buttering the mold or lining it with plastic wrap) to be sure that the food will be able to be removed from the mold later. Silicone is a more modern mold material, and has the benefit of being able to withstand a wide range of high and low temperatures, as well as being physically flexible enough to twist and turn inside out, easily ejecting the food when the time comes. The ice cube tray (opposite page) is a simple example of a mold.

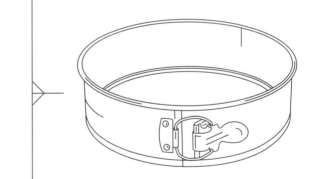

Everything in Its Place

Mise en place—the French culinary term meaning "everything in its place"—is a way to organize one's kitchen and the food and equipment in it with the goal of increasing one's ability to cook food on the fly. Literally, this is interpreted as measuring, cleaning, and processing all of your ingredients ahead of time so that one can assemble and cook a dish without needing to pause until it is completed. The thinking behind this concept is that by having each necessary item at one's fingertips—including everything from raw ingredients to any pre-assembled parts of a dish like a complicated sauce or homemade pasta—one can execute a dish with increased ease and speed. Having a complete and thorough mise en place is the only way restaurants are able to put out food in such large quantities, especially with recipes that cumulatively take hours to make. In addition, the lack of this sort of careful planning can result in disruptions to cooking that may have negative effects on the final dish. Any missteps of timing in an especially calibrated dish like a stir-fry, where cooking is sometimes counted in seconds, can cause ingredients to overcook or over reduce, and the end result could easily be a ruinous mess. In fact, Chinese cooking is one cuisine where most chefs agree a mise en place is totally necessary, even in home kitchens. That said, while mise en place can be very helpful in specific kitchens and for cooking specific dishes, many other meals, especially those made in the leisure of a home kitchen, can get by with careful and thoughtful prepping and cleaning as you go.

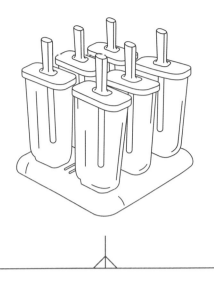

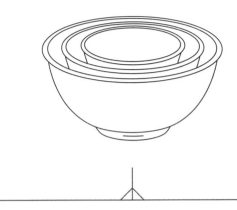

POPSICLE MOLDS

Popsicle molds are plastic, silicone, or thin metal vessels that are filled with fruit puree or custard and placed into the freezer; when frozen solid, the filling forms into popsicles that can then be removed and eaten. Like an ice cube tray (page 100), popsicle molds come in a variety of sizes and shapes—including cylinder shapes with rounded bottoms or paddle shapes—and usually contain at least four cavities that can be filled. Some varieties include a lid for the molds that has slots where popsicle sticks may be inserted and held vertically, suspended in the liquid until it freezes; without this stabilizing lid, the popsicle sticks have a tendency to fall to the side of the cavity. To remove the finished frozen popsicles from the mold, dip the mold into warm or hot water for a moment; the exterior of the popsicles should melt just enough to release them from the container.

PREP BOWLS

In the same category as mixing bowls, prep bowls are multi-size vessels used to hold ingredients after they have been "prepped" but before they have been cooked or combined with other items. Perhaps made more popular by the proliferation of televised cooking shows, where hosts keep ingredients that have been previously cleaned, cut, and measured in prep bowls until they're ready to be added to a recipe, these bowls are key to creating one's mise en place (see Everything in Its Place, opposite page). They hold chopped, mashed, or otherwise processed ingredients—washed and minced parsley, sifted flour, or beaten eggs, for example—that have been measured out and are ready to add to a waiting mixing bowl, pan, pot, or other cooking or serving vessel. Some prep bowls are more utilitarian than others, with standard measurements etched into the sides. Many prep bowls also come in sets that nest together for easy storage. Glass versions are popular as they allow the cook to clearly see the contents of each bowl, but ceramic, plastic, and silicone options are also available. Other small bowls like ramekins (page 132) can be substituted as needed.

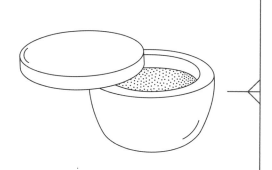

SALT CELLAR

A salt cellar, also called a salt pig or salt box, is a vessel made for holding and dispensing salt. There are multiple sizes: large versions for the kitchen that allow a cook to reach in with one hand to grab salt and season food as it cooks, as well as small versions used on the table. Most options require the use of one's hand to pinch and remove the salt from the cellar, though some formal, individualized versions used on the table sometimes have a tiny spoon included. Styles range from open topped vessels—some with a hood half covering the top, some without—to lidded options. Most are made from humble ceramic, wood, or metal, though some tabletop versions are also made from silver or silver plate and can be quite ornate. The benefit of a salt cellar lies in the control it offers a cook over the amounts of salt used in a dish. Pouring salt out of a box is unreliable and using measuring spoons (page 110) isn't always sensible (especially given how much food is seasoned "to taste"). Using a salt cellar encourages chefs and home cooks alike to acquire the ability to pinch the right amount using only their tactile senses, which is an easier, more efficient method of seasoning a dish.

The Cleanliness of (Salt) Pigs

By name alone, the salt pig (also known as a salt cellar) invokes a greedy image, and the fact that one's hands are often the tool of choice when removing salt from its gaping maw adds to the potentially unseemly connotations of this kitchen staple. And what if the hands in question aren't sparkling clean? Luckily the substance one is grabbing is salt—a natural preservative that will kill most bacteria—so the contents of the salt pig will likely be, and remain, contaminant free. However, to be on the safe side, when seasoning foods that need to be handled carefully due to potential salmonella (like raw chicken) or other bacteria, be sure to dispense a portion of salt into a ramekin (page 132) or another small container before beginning the cooking process. Then, when it comes time to season, draw from the stand-in vessel instead of the main salt supply housed inside the salt pig, thereby avoiding any cross contamination.

Measuring Devices

When exactness is necessary, certain kitchen tools take the guess work out of a food's temperature and weight. In baking especially, precision regarding the amounts of sugar, flour, and other ingredients can make or break a recipe, so a scale is often necessary. On the process side, thermometers and timers are just as vital, as they can indicate the exact status of cooking.

CANDY THERMOMETER

A candy thermometer is a temperature-taking device made specifically for the cooking of sugar. In addition to being marked with Celsius and Fahrenheit temperatures, it is often marked with the various stages of candy making, including the soft ball, hard ball, soft crack, and hard crack stages, among others, which correspond to the various ways that cooked sugar will react when heated to these ranges of temperature. The thermometer often includes a clip that will attach it to the side of a pot, making it easy for the bulb of the thermometer to remain submerged in the pot without touching the bottom; clipping it to the pot also enables a continuous read on the temperature, as sugar can burn quickly.

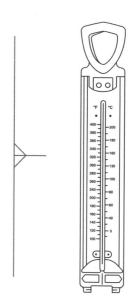

MEASURING CUPS

A measuring cup is a vessel that holds a standard measurement, usually ranging from a ¼ cup to 2 cups. There are two types. A dry measuring cup, often made of metal, plastic, or ceramic, with a short handle for ease of use, has a single-amount design: a 1-cup measure holds exactly that amount when it is filled and leveled off with a knife or straight edge. This type of measuring cup is often sold in sets that include a few sizes (for example, a starter set might include a ¼ cup, ⅓ cup, ½ cup, and 1 cup), and the cups nestle inside one another for convenience. The other type of measuring cup is a liquid measuring cup in the form of a glass or plastic cup with a handle and spout, with marked gradations on the transparent sides to indicate escalating amounts, say, from ¼ cup to as much as 8 cups. To use, the cook pours in the ingredient until it reaches the demarcation that indicates the correct amount.

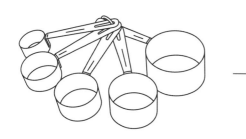

Methods for Measuring

Cooks and bakers mostly agree that when using a set of dry measurement cups, one should overfill the cup as called for and then level it off using a straight edge. What is not agreed on is the method of filling the cups. Some dip their measuring cups directly into a container holding their desired ingredient and scoop up the product. Others spoon an ingredient from its original container into their individual measuring cup until the cup is overflowing. Still others prefer to pack an ingredient into a measuring cup, pushing in as much as possible. In addition, some cooks sift dry ingredients prior to measuring, while others do not. It is no surprise that these methods of filling a measuring cup can create differences in aeration and density that result in widely varying "cups" of sugar, salt, flour, and other commonly measured ingredients. Some cookbook authors, especially bakers, make note of their method of measuring, so that the reader can do the same. If this direction is given, use it, as the recipes in the book will have been tested to that specification. If this information is not provided, the stir and scoop method is popular and offers a good middle ground. First, stir the dry ingredient to be measured but do not sift it. This aerates the ingredient slightly so it is not too densely packed. Next, scoop the ingredient gently using the measuring cup and make sure to include an excessive heap that spills over the top of the cup. Finally, level off the excess mound with a knife or other straight-edged implement. If you find this level of precise imprecision to still be a bother, make the switch to metric (weighted) measurements, if the cookbook provides them. Weighing your ingredients means your measurements will always be correct, leaving no room for interpretation.

MEASURING SPOONS

Similar to measuring cups but used for smaller amounts, a measuring spoon holds a standard small measurement in volume. Holding anywhere from a dash to a tablespoon (page 161), measuring spoons come in a set with several size capacities and nestle inside one another: ¼ teaspoon, ½ teaspoon, 1 teaspoon, and 1 tablespoon are common measures included in a set.

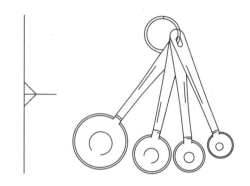

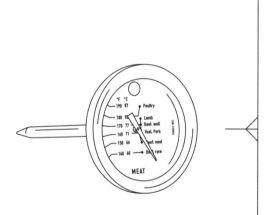

MEAT THERMOMETER

A meat thermometer is a temperature-taking device made specifically for the cooking of meat. There are a couple of different styles. The traditional version is an analog temperature dial mounted onto a probe that is inserted into a roast, burger, or other piece of cooking meat. With this type, temperature is taken on an as-needed basis only. More contemporary meat thermometer probes connect to a digital display via wire or wirelessly (by pushing information to an app on a cell phone). This version can be inserted into the meat for its cooking duration, and usually can sound an alarm when a certain temperature is reached.

Temperature-Taking Techniques

A cook often relies on a thermometer to help tell if a food is cooked enough that it is safe to eat (often meat), or enough that it will behave as planned in a dish (often sugar). In these cases, precision is paramount, so be sure when inserting the probe that it is centered in the food: not on the surface (which will be hotter), nor touching the sides or bottom of a hot pan or pot. When temping meat, the probe should also not touch any large bones, which conduct heat differently and will give an incorrect reading; if you touch bone with the probe, pull back on it or insert it again elsewhere so it will read the temperature of the flesh only.

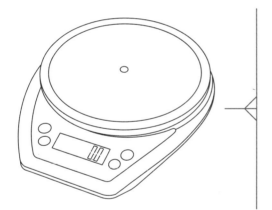

SCALE

A kitchen scale is a weight-measuring device made specifically for food, especially spices and any other dry goods. While measuring cups and spoons (page 108 and opposite page) rely on volume, and are sufficient for some recipes, others, especially for baked goods, need the accuracy of weight to guarantee success. Most scales these days are digital, and include a tare button to "zero out" the weight of a waiting bowl or vessel in preparation for the next ingredient to be weighed.

TIMER

A timer, sometimes called a kitchen timer or egg timer, is an analog or digital device that counts down cooking time for the chef. Many dishes in the kitchen, especially baked goods, require exact prep or cooking time, so a timer is useful. Some are attached to a magnet so it can be stuck to the fridge or other appliances. Professional kitchens often have multiple timers for various projects going at once.

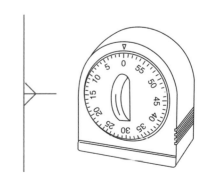

Textiles

One cannot forget about the pots and pans that are required for cooking and baking, but there are also a variety of cloth items that make food prep easier. Ranging in purpose from safety, as in oven mitts and pot holders, to cleanliness, textiles help a kitchen run smoothly and neatly.

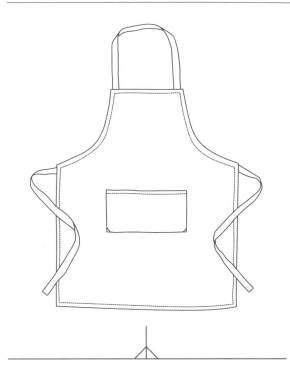

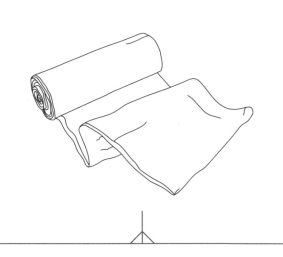

APRON

The primary purpose of an apron is to protect a food handler's clothing from stains, smears, and splatter, and is used by professional chefs, waitstaff, and home cooks. They come in two formats: the bib apron, which hangs from the neck and covers the full front of the body, or the waist apron, which ties around one's middle to offer protection from the waist down. Made of cloth, plastic, or even leather, most aprons tie at the back (which prevents the ends from dangling into food or flame), although front-tie or Japanese cross-back versions (which requires no tying at all) are also popular choices. In addition to protecting one's clothes and body, an apron often includes pockets, which are very helpful for tucking in pens, notepads, hand towels, corkscrews, or anything else a cook or server must have on hand.

CHEESECLOTH

A cheesecloth is a reusable, woven piece of fabric through which foods are strained or wrapped around ingredients and added to a liquid to flavor it without leaving behind any debris, such as a bouquet garni (a collection of herbs and spices wrapped in cheesecloth and tied with kitchen string) in a simmering stock or stew. Cheesecloth is also used to line a colander when separating liquids from fine solids, such as when making cheese and nut milks. It can also be helpful as a very fine strainer by passing fruit juices, custards, and more through it to achieve a very smooth final product. Cheesecloth is typically made from light, gauze-like cotton and is available in a variety of different grades, from an open to an extra-fine weave, which indicate the thread count.

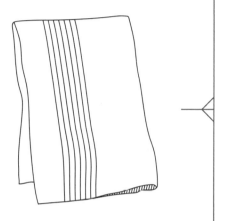

KITCHEN TOWEL

The kitchen towel, or dish towel (or moppine, in some Neapolitan-American circles), is intended for many functions in the kitchen, ranging from wiping up and absorbing spills, cleaning and drying surfaces, drying hands, swiping messy serving plates, and even handling hot pots and dishes. Usually made from thick cotton and in a variety of styles (from nondescript to themed), the kitchen towel is meant to be tougher and stronger than the average bath towel and is used by chefs, home cooks, and waitstaff.

Hands Off

Because of its multiple uses, kitchen towels should be washed often to avoid cross contamination. A towel that has been used to wipe down a cutting board after butchering a chicken should obviously not be used to dry clean hands; a towel used to dry dishes should never be used to then remove a hot pan from the oven, as the moisture in the wet towel will conduct the heat and burn your hand. As such, professionals notoriously guard their extra kitchen towels closely, as they replace them multiple times a day and towels are somewhat rationed in professional kitchens.

KITCHEN TWINE

Kitchen twine, a food-safe cotton string, is a multipurpose tool in the kitchen. The plain undyed version is most often used to tie up roasts, truss birds, or bundle herbs for a soup or stew (as in a bouquet garni). Once its task is complete, the twine is removed and discarded prior to serving. More decorative twine—often thinner and sometimes candy striped and referred to as baker's twine—is used for packaging baked goods, tying around boxes or jars, and securing the tops of bags. When buying kitchen twine, do not purchase any string that contains synthetics. Kitchen twine does not contain any inedible dyes or additives, and will not melt or burn in the oven. Silicone ties, which are reusable, are becoming available as a substitute to kitchen twine, but they lack the versatility of this simple tool.

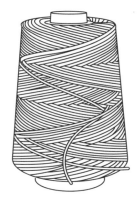

Knots for Every Occasion

When using kitchen twine, particular knots can be employed in certain cooking situations to help the twine do its particular job. A butchers' knot is a type of slip knot that is easily adjustable (especially with one set of hands); it is therefore best for cinching together a rolled-up piece of meat. While a baker may use various decorative knots to secure boxes and bags, a simple square knot is just fine in most situations.

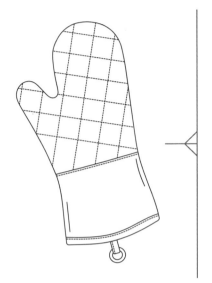

OVEN MITT

An oven mitt is a padded heatproof glove that protects a cook's hands from hot bakeware, pots, and pans, and provides enough grip to move these hot vessels to or from the oven or stovetop. The oven mitt is shaped like a large mitten (it's always one size fits all) with a compartment for one's thumb and another for four fingers, and is typically made from a durable, thick, quilted cotton that has been lined with a heat insulator. More contemporary versions might include or be made entirely from silicone. Styles vary, but the safest oven mitt is one that gives the most coverage—the best choice is a mitt that extends partway up your arm, allowing you to safely reach deep into your oven.

POT HOLDER

Similar to the oven mitt, a pot holder is a thick square pad used to protect one's hands when handling hot kitchen equipment. Unlike the oven-mitt, the pot holder is not a glove or mitten, but rather a simple cloth barrier between the hand and the pot; that said, some pot holders do have a pocket for the tip of one's hand. Usually made from a thick, quilted or woven cotton (though occasionally silicone will be used as well), pot holders are about the size of a hand so as not to be too cumbersome to be helpful.

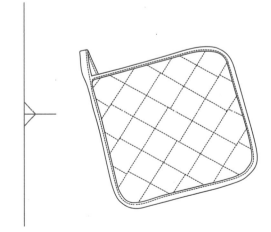

Work Surfaces

CARVING BOARD

COOLING RACK

CUTTING BOARD

DISH DRYING RACK

PASTA DRYING RACK

PASTRY BOARD

There are active prep tools, such as mortars and pestles or knives, and then there are passive tools, like these work surfaces. Both are necessary for kitchen prep.

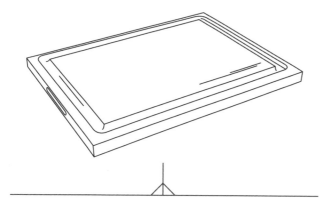

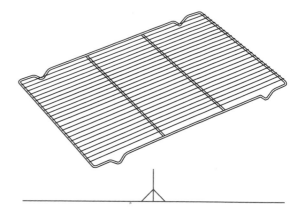

CARVING BOARD

A carving board is a special type of large cutting surface that is made specifically for carving roasts and other large cooked meats. Made of wood, a carving board is different from a standard cutting board because it has channels etched into the horizontal cutting surface which both drain and collect the juices from the meat being sliced. These channels can be as simple in design as a groove running around the perimeter of the board, or they can include a more ornate labyrinth of channels that work to send liquid from the center of the board to a corner indentation. Not only do these channels prevent a mess from forming—otherwise these juices will trickle off the cutting board and onto the countertop or table—but they also allow a cook to access this flavorful liquid, making it easy to spoon the juices back over the meat or pour into a gravy boat (page 172). A carving board also differs from a cutting board in that it can also be used for serving, and thus can include more ornate and decorative designs like metal or silver handles attached to the sides of the board, allowing for ease in transferring to a buffet or tabletop.

COOLING RACK

A cooling rack is an elevated horizontal grid of metal wire meant to hold cookies, cakes, bread, and other hot-from-the-oven items as they cool. The added height of the rack helps air circulate beneath as well as around the item, ensuring that it doesn't steam and get soggy as it cools.

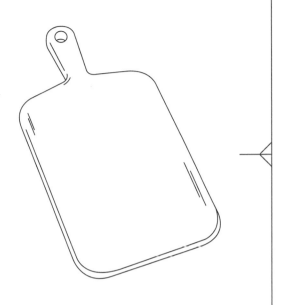

CUTTING BOARD

A cutting board is a portable surface meant for cutting, chopping, and prepping ingredients. A wooden cutting board, the most common type, has the benefit of being a soft enough substance so as to not damage a knife's edge, but still strong, hard, and rigid enough to withstand the chopping or cutting being done on its surface. Plastic cutting boards are convenient for ingredients that might require the board to be disinfected after, such as raw poultry, as they can be washed thoroughly or even put in a dishwasher. Cutting boards can also be made of glass, steel, or marble, which have varying levels of effectiveness. Having more than one type of cutting board can be convenient depending on the cook's needs.

DISH DRYING RACK

A dish drying rack is a plastic, metal, or wooden rack meant to hold dishes, glassware, and kitchen equipment after washing, eliminating the need for active drying. The rack usually sits on the counter next to the sink, and can include an attached container for holding smaller items such as utensils and/or design elements especially made for holding glasses upside down. A dish drying rack is often accompanied by a drain board, a flat surface that sits below the dish rack at a small incline, meant to capture the dripping water of the drying dishes and funnel it back into the sink.

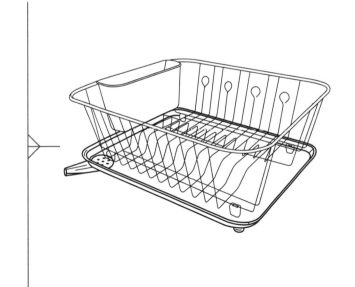

PASTA DRYING RACK

A pasta drying rack is a resting place for homemade long cut pasta, such as spaghetti or linguine. Just-made fresh pasta can stick to itself right after being cut; a rack is necessary to spread out and hold the pasta so that air can flow through the strands and they can dry a bit prior to cooking. Often constructed from a collection of dowels attached to a stand, the rack's arms are horizontal, splayed out so one can drape the finished pasta over them.

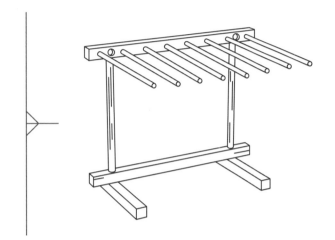

Rack Alternatives

If one does not have a pasta drying rack, there are other household items that can step in to save the day. A laundry drying rack is a very similar contraption, just on a larger scale—it will hold all the pasta a home cook might make. Clothes hangers can function similarly to the dowels: just load and hang. The back of a (clean) kitchen chair works too. Or don't hang it all: just toss the fresh pasta with a bit of extra flour and spread it out in a single layer on a kitchen towel—there will be less air circulation, but the result will be about the same.

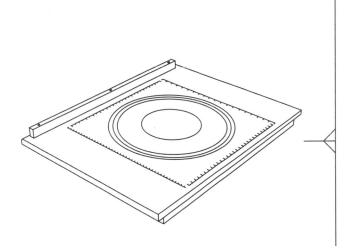

PASTRY BOARD

A pastry board, also known as a bread board, is a portable horizontal surface specially made for kneading, cutting, and rolling out pastry, bread, or pasta dough. Made of wood or marble, a pastry board is differentiated from a cutting board by its built-in lip that hangs over the edge of a countertop, providing extra stability, even when manipulating and pressing ingredients on it. (Some have two lips, making the board reversible.) Versions also include measurements and concentric circles of varying sizes which can be helpful when rolling out crusts. Marble pastry boards have the added benefit of being cold to the touch, which is helpful when making pastry doughs that need to be kept cool.

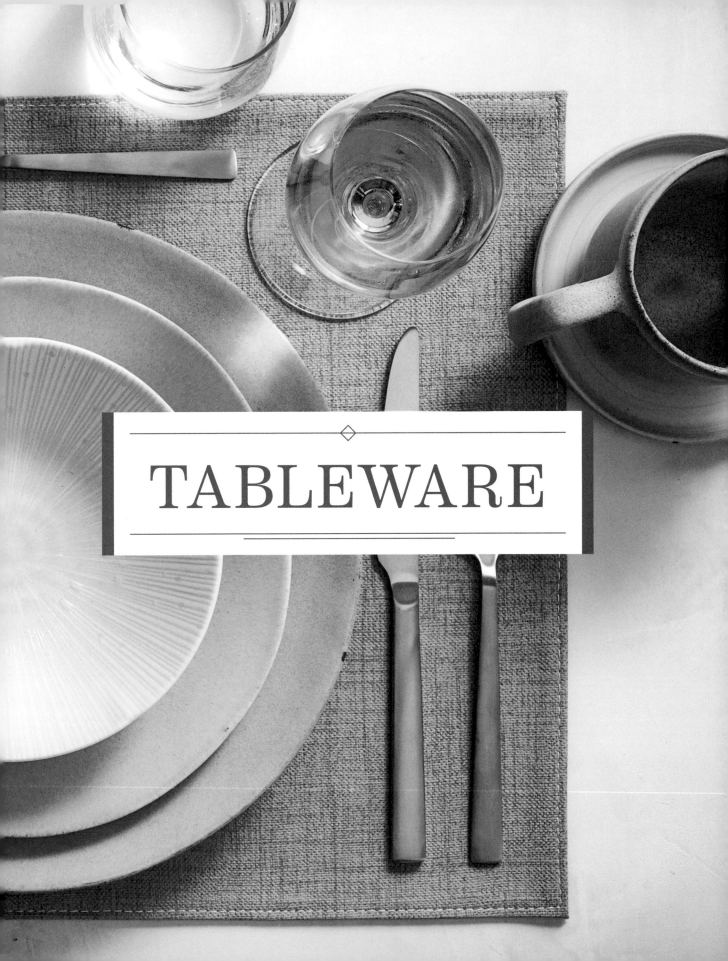

TABLEWARE

Dinnerware

As opposed to serving dishes, which are used for presenting food, eating dishes are ones meant for individual use. This is a formality familiar now, but in poorer or more informal cultures and in the past, having one's own reusable eating surface (as opposed to a communal dish, or even a natural "plate," like a leaf) would be considered very special indeed. For ease of reference in this text, we've chosen to call these pieces dinnerware, but they are used for all meals. These days, there is a wide selection of these type of dishes, which range from the multipurpose, like a plate, to the more obscure or specific, like an eggcup. Dinnerware is often merchandized and sold as sets with varying inclusion.

BOWL

A bowl is a concave dish or container that is used to store, prepare, and serve food. With a rounded interior, bowls are particularly ideal for holding liquid or loose foods, with a low, centered focus of gravity collecting the food. A bowl is one of the earliest dishes known to man, and it was used in many cultures around the world. Modern bowls are typically made of ceramic, glass, metal, wood, or plastic, depending on their size and use, but stone was used historically. In addition to being found at a table setting as an individual's dish, bowls can also be used to mix ingredients (page 100) and to serve large communal dishes like salad or soup.

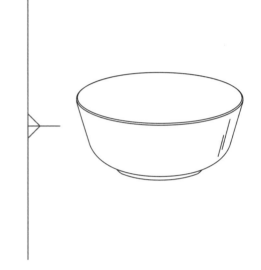

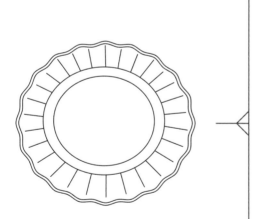

BREAD-AND-BUTTER PLATE

Followed by the salad plate (page 132) and the dessert plate (page 130), the bread-and-butter plate is the smallest side plate that is included in a formal place setting with any kind of regularity. On the table, this plate is placed above the dinner plate (page 131) and to the left, and is often set with an accompanying butter knife (page 150). As formal dinnerware sets become less popular, and as fewer hosts automatically give their guests a serving of bread and butter, this plate might be considered extraneous by some. Like all of the dishes in a place setting set, these are most often made of porcelain or other ceramic material.

Bowled Over

Because of their generous holding capacity and their raised sides, bowls are the perfect containers for serving and eating a wide variety of foods that have a sauce or are liquid. So it's no surprise that there are many different types of bowls with varying shapes and sizes, as well as specialized designs invented for specific tasks. While you can rely on the fact that a set of dishes will almost always include a bowl (opposite page), what type of bowl is included depends on the buyer, the location, and the brand. Usually there are a few options. Traditional soup bowls are small, shallow bowls without a lip, and with two looped handles attached. These are much more common in older, more formal sets of china. A more modern version of the soup bowl, sometimes called a soup "plate," is comprised of a flatter, shallow bowl with a wide rim. Cereal bowls are also more contemporary offerings: smaller in diameter (similar to a soup bowl) but with a deep concavity and steep sides, making them better able to hold milk. Similar in capacity to soup "plates" are pasta bowls, which are large, shallow bowls that offer no lip or handles. As opposed to a plate, which might not be able to contain a looser sauce, a pasta bowl's slightly raised sides will hold an entire dish together and might even keep it hotter longer. Always popular in Italy, pasta bowls are becoming increasingly available in other countries (especially the US) as pasta becomes more of a staple food. Rice bowls are deep, small bowls without a lip, similar to a cereal bowl, but more diminutive in size. These bowls are a must in China, Japan, and many other Asian countries. In some cases, a rice bowl will be the only individual dish for eating: one's serving of rice in the bowl acts as a base for combining with bites of various foods and accoutrements that are meant for sharing and thus served from communal dishes.

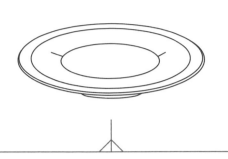

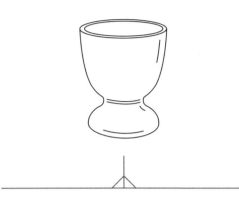

DESSERT PLATE

The dessert plate, a common inclusion in any formal place setting, is an individual-use, medium-size plate made specifically for serving dessert. It is a similar size like the salad plate (page 132), and in a pinch could be used interchangeably—though Emily Post and her followers would certainly frown upon this. Sometimes a dessert plate is more highly decorated than a salad plate. Some believe this extra ornamentation is because dessert is the last chance to impress your guests before the end of dinner; it may also be because dessert has to stand alone after the rest of the table has been cleared, so extra decoration would stand out. Dessert plates, like all of the dishes in a set, are most often made of porcelain or other ceramic material.

EGGCUP

An eggcup is a small rounded cup used to hold a boiled egg in its shell. The egg sits flush in the cup, leaving the top half of the egg exposed; to eat, the top of the shell is sliced off and the egg is scooped out of the shell with a spoon. Eggcups are made out of any number of materials, including glass, wood, ceramic, and plastic, and can come in sets to accommodate multiple people at a breakfast table.

A Classic Eggcup Pairing

In traditional Western breakfasts, eggs and toast go together. Eggs prepared for eating out of eggcups are often softboiled and buttered toast is regularly an accompaniment. While a full piece of toast is fine, upping the ante to toast "soldiers" means that the thin strips of toast will fit nicely into the eggshell, making it easy enough to dip into the yolk of the egg while it sits in its cup.

Edible Eating Dishes

There are multiple foods that came into existence because of the fact you did not need a dish to eat them: the original convenience foods. Sandwiches hold the most nutritious and interesting foods in an inexpensive but filling wrapper, bread. Same goes for tortillas, with tacos, burritos, and other stuffed dishes. Pasties are pastries made in the UK filled with ingredients and sealed into a pocket and eaten out of hand. In Japan, rice is sometimes wrapped in seaweed so that it can easily be eaten with your hands. So despite there being many options, dishes are not always needed!

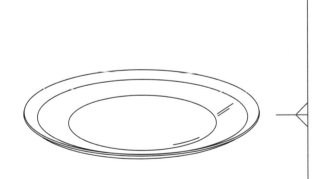

PLATE

A plate is a flat dish on which an individual meal is served. They usually have a slight concavity to hold the food in place, and can be any shape, though circular plates are the most common. Plates are made out of a wide variety of materials, including metal, plastic, ceramic, wood, glass, and even paper, which will be disposable. In sets of china, plates are the most important piece, and have multiple variations depending on the extravagance of the set—ranging in purpose from dinner plate to serving platter to cup saucer, salad plate (page 132), and dessert plate (opposite page).

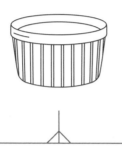

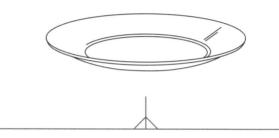

RAMEKIN

A ramekin is a small glazed ceramic or glass bowl, used for cooking and also for serving. Ramekins hold 2 to 8 fluid ounces each, and are used to prepare and serve single servings, some of which are cooked in the ramekin, like baked eggs, French onion soup, crème brûlée, and molten chocolate cake. Because of their small size, they can also be used to serve olives or nuts, or can be packed with paté or potted shrimp. A ramekin is able to withstand high heat: the oven, the broiler, or a kitchen torch. Because the food is also served in the ramekin it was cooked in, ramekins can be decorative, though the most common ramekins are circular with straight sides, in white ceramic with a fluted texture on the outside walls. Certain recipes require the food being turned out of the ramekin prior to serving, in which case the food often retains the puck-like shape of the original dish.

SALAD PLATE

Traditionally, the salad plate is used for eating salad either before or after the main course. In a formal place setting, it sits either on top of the dinner plate, placed at the upper left of the dinner plate, or is filled in the kitchen and brought to the table. Due to their inherent formality, salad plates are typically porcelain, but can also be metal, plastic, or wood; like plates, they can be plain or highly decorated. Though not intended to do so, one can use a salad plate for dessert instead, as the sizes are almost indistinguishable.

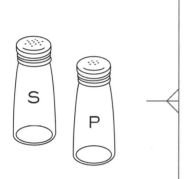

SALT & PEPPER SHAKERS

Salt and pepper shakers are small containers—often communal, but occasionally individual—which hold salt and ground black pepper; to use them, the diner turns them upside down to sprinkle salt and pepper over their food for additional seasoning. Often sold in sets, salt and pepper shakers can be made of glass, plastic, metal, or ceramic, and can come in simple or classic styles, as well as ornate and even novelty designs, often featuring pairs, like two of the same animal, or classic duos like a king and queen. Sometimes the only way to distinguish which shaker holds salt and which holds pepper is by the number of holes at the top: in the US, the shaker with fewer holes is for the salt (confusingly, in the UK, the piece with the fewer holes contains the pepper). A pepper grinder (page 221) is an alternative to a pepper shaker.

Not Just Salt

———○———

A restaurant's salt shaker will sometimes include rice, but have no concerns about the establishment's sanitary practices. A few grains of raw rice added to a shaker helps keep the salt from caking, allowing it to flow smoothly.

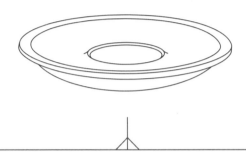

SAUCER

A saucer is a shallow underplate meant to hold a teacup, coffee cup, or espresso cup. The size of a saucer corresponds with the size of the cup it holds (a saucer for an espresso cup will be more petite than a saucer for a coffee cup), but in general this dish is smaller than a bread-and-butter plate (page 128), and is likely to be the smallest flat piece of china in a set. Design-wise, what distinguishes the saucer from other plates is the circular indentation in the center of the plate, where its corresponding cup should fit exactly. In addition to holding its cup upright—which is helpful as some cups (especially teacups) have narrow bottoms that tip easily—the saucer is also helpful in catching any liquid that might dribble down the outside edge of the cup after a sip is taken, thus protecting the table or tablecloth from staining; it can also hold a small spoon that has been soiled by stirring milk or sugar into a drink. The saucer also provides a further layer of protection for the table, otherwise the hot cup of liquid could leave a ring, as wood is very heat sensitive and prone to this type of damage. In the eighteenth and nineteenth century, some tea and coffee drinkers—including Thomas Jefferson most famously—drank directly from the saucer. The thinking was that by pouring portions of any hot beverage out of their cups and into a saucer, the flatter dish would let off more steam due to its increased exposed surface area, and quickly cool the drink.

China Galore

Just as there is a wide variety of historical and modern flatware available (see Utensils of Yore, page 151), the possible inclusions in a set of china can vary tremendously. Typical modern sets of china usually include a four- or five-piece place setting—a dinner plate, a bowl of some kind, a salad/dessert plate, and a mug or teacup with a saucer. A bread-and-butter plate is another relatively common inclusion in most standard china sets. However, if money is no object, a set can be comprised of hundreds of different dishes, depending on the number of settings and the specialty pieces chosen. In addition to the four- or five-piece sets mentioned above, an individual setting could also have a charger, which is the largest of all plates and acts as a decorative underplate that is not used for serving actual food. In addition, some sets include individual lunch or breakfast dishes, which are generally smaller-size plates and bowls meant for these less formal meals. The serving dishes can also vary widely, from dishes made to contain very specific or obscure foods, as well as the most grandiose presentation pieces created, scaled, and decorated for maximum visual impact.

In comparison, serving plates, serving bowls, and platters are fairly common, but they still come in a variety of sizes and shapes and even they are sometimes designed exclusively for certain meats, fish, vegetables, and desserts. Pitchers (for drinks or soups) and gravy boats (page 172) are relatively popular as most people (in the US, at least) tend to use their "good china" over the holidays, when roasts with their accompanying sauces or gravies are customarily eaten. Tureens, used for soups or stews, tend to be the biggest pieces of any set, and they often come with ornate lids. Coffee and/or tea service comprise another subset of dishes that can include teapots, coffee urns, sugar bowls, creamers, cups (from teacups to coffee cups to espresso cups), saucers, mugs, and trays. Butter dishes, olive dishes, relish dishes, mustard pots, cake stands, holders for toothpicks, salt shakers or cellars, tea caddies, punch bowls and cups, finger bowls (tiny bowls into which the diner is expected to carefully dip their fingers to clean them), and even rare items like snuff boxes can be found, especially in older English china sets, which are available mostly in antique shops and online.

Drinkware

Vessels to drink from take a variety of forms, and one can argue that the shape and size of a glass has a real impact on the taste of the drink inside. Bartenders say that each glass has an intended drink, and would never serve an Old Fashioned in a champagne coupe. Follow their lead if you wish, or focus in on just a couple of multipurpose glasses for your drinking needs.

CHAMPAGNE GLASS

The Champagne glass, formal ware used to drink champagne, can come in one of three shapes: the flute, the coupe, and the tulip. The champagne flute is the most common type, with a long stem tapering out into a tall, thin glass bowl. The shape of the bowl and the texture of the bottom cause bubbles to constantly rise to the top of the drink, which release more flavor and aroma and create an impressive visual. The old-fashioned champagne coupe has a very short and wide bowl, which may be one reason why it is less popular today, as its design causes bubbles to dissipate quickly. Lastly, the tulip is similar to the shape of the flute, but has a slight bulge around the middle of the bowl. This is an increasingly popular style among professionals as its slightly tapered top tends to collect aromas rather than letting them dissappate, unlike the flute, and remains narrow enough to retain the carbonation, unlike the coupe.

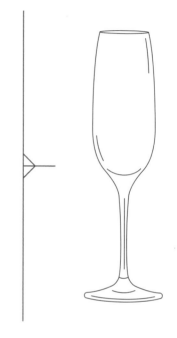

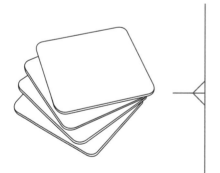

COASTER

A trivet for a glass, a coaster is a piece of material used to protect the surface of a wood or marble table or bar. A drink's condensation and temperature can make potentially permanent rings on a surface, so a coaster placed beneath each glass can prevent this. They are used for any type of drink, hot or cold, whether served in a mug, glass, or bottle, and can be made from cork, wood, stone, ceramic, and so on.

COUPE

The coupe—a long-stemmed glass with a very short, broad bowl—was the original design for champagne in the mid-seventeenth century. But the design of the coupe made it not ideal for champagne's fizziness, as its wide mouth let the carbonation dissipate before the glass was finished. So in the present day, this glass is used primarily for non-carbonated drinks like martinis, which are strong enough to come in the small portion a coupe can hold.

Coaster Evolution

Coasters have evolved from being merely functional to being a canvas for messages. Bars and pubs will usually have paper or cardboard coasters, known as beermats, scattered around their space to protect their tables and bar. Cheap to create, these coasters are often emblazoned with the bar's logo or advertisements, increasing brand recognition for the establishment.

DECANTER

Originally, a decanter was a serving vessel for wine, where the wine, when ready to drink, was carefully poured into the decanter to separate it from the settled sediment in the bottom of the original bottle. Modern wines have much less sediment, and so decanting is less necessary (and common) than it was in Ancient Rome. Another benefit of using a decanter is the aeration the wine receives when being transferred from the original bottle to the decanter. A decanter, which often has a stopper included, is usually made of crystal or glass, and these days can be used for wine or as a decorative bottle for any other liquors in a home bar, like whiskey or scotch.

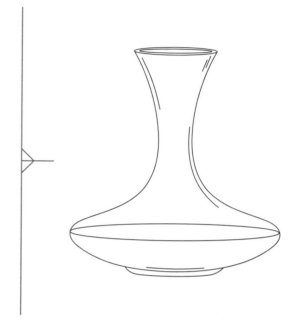

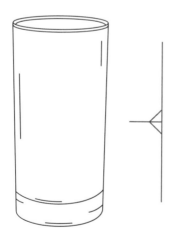

HIGHBALL GLASS

A highball glass is a tall skinny tumbler used to serve highball cocktails, mixed drinks served over ice with a hearty amount of mixer (like a rum and coke or gin and tonic), which necessitates a larger, taller glass to accommodate the drink's proportions. Perhaps the largest glass in a bar, the highball is also often used as a water or mocktail glass.

MARTINI GLASS

A martini glass is a type of cocktail glass with an iconic inverted cone-shaped bowl, set on a thin tall stem. It serves a variety of straight-up cocktails—meaning that the drink was shaken with ice but is not served with or over ice—such as the eponymous martini, gimlet, Cosmopolitan, and Manhattan, among many others. The stem guarantees one's hands will not warm the chilled drink, and the wide bowl showcases the aromatics of the ingredients.

MUG

A ceramic cup usually with a handle to protect one's hands from the heat, a mug is less formal than a traditional teacup, but serves the same general purpose as an individual vessel to hold hot liquid. While glass mugs exist, the much more common ceramic versions' relatively thick sides insulate the liquid, keeping it hotter longer. In addition to holding hot drinks of any kind, mugs can also be used for soup. Travel mugs are often made of insulated metal or plastic for durability.

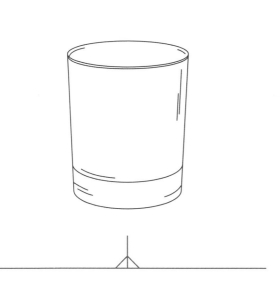

OLD FASHIONED GLASS

Also called a lowball glass, the Old Fashioned glass is a short, wide cocktail tumbler. The glass is used to make cocktails such as the Old Fashioned, of course, which requires ingredients to be added and treated before the liquor is added. In the case of the Old Fashioned, a sugar cube, a dash of bitters, and a splash of water must be muddled together prior to the whiskey and ice being added. The wide rim and short height of the glass, along with its thick base, are designs catered to muddling. The small Old Fashioned glass is also often the glass of choice for unmixed drinks, with just liquor served either neat (no ice) or on the rocks (over ice).

PITCHER

Also called a jug, a pitcher is used to decant liquid, most often into individual glasses. In most cases this is a beverage, though sauces and soups, especially cold ones, can be served from a pitcher. Shape and size vary: one can have a small pitcher, best used for syrup for pancakes, for example, or a large pitcher, ideal for providing iced tea to a group. Many have handles, though not strictly necessary, and all have spouts. Style and materials range from porcelain to glass, metal, or plastic. Some pitchers include a lid so they may be safely stored in the refrigerator; some lids feature perforated sides which, when rotated toward a pitcher's spout, allows the pourer to choose whether to strain the drink as you pour (to keep ice cubes in the pitcher, perhaps) or to pour freely.

SAMOVAR

In Russian, samovar translates to "self-brewer," which explains the purpose of this large metal pot that heats and boils water. Thought to be more than 3,000 years old, traditional samovars were heated with coal or charcoal at the base; more modern models function similarly to an electric water kettle, plugging into the wall in order to heat the water. They are found in many countries in Europe, the Middle East, and Asia. A samovar is traditionally metal, made out of iron, copper, nickel, brass, tin, or more expensive metals like silver and gold. More ornate versions are often engraved, embossed, or coated in enamel. Some samovars have attachments that hold tea, allowing it to brew in the container.

SHOT GLASS

A shot glass is a very small glass with a heavy bottom and steep sloping sides. It holds only a single portion of straight liquor. The exact amount a shot glass can hold varies considerably, especially depending on the country; double shot glasses hold twice as much. One is normally expected to "shoot"—or drink—the whole amount at once. Shot glasses can also be used as a measuring device when making cocktails.

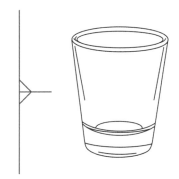

SNIFTER

Also known as a brandy snifter or cognac glass, a snifter is a short-stemmed drinking glass with a low, wide bowl that tapers to a small opening on top, usually used to serve small amounts of neat dark spirits. The design aims to evaporate the liquid by allowing it to spread out over a larger surface area while retaining the aroma, though some argue the trapped alcohol aroma can get so strong that it can kill your palate. The bulbous cup fits into the palm of one's hand, allowing the drinker to subtly warm the liquor with body heat. This shape of glass also emphasizes the aromas of dark, aromatic beers.

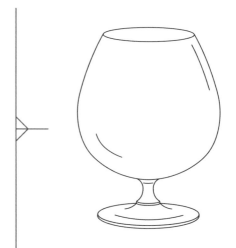

Drinking Glass Conundrums

While most glasses have specific names that help identify them—highball, cocktail, coupe—a "drinking glass" designation can seem both redundant and overly general. Most can agree this glass is meant for everyday drinking; however, its style and design can vary widely, encompassing everything from tall, etched options to more squat, family-friendly vessels. Drinking glasses usually have a lot in common with highball glasses (page 140), as they are big enough to really quench one's thirst. That said, some might define drinking glasses simply as the everyday vessel from which one drinks, even if that vessel is a repurposed jam jar.

TEACUP

A teacup is a small porcelain or ceramic cup meant to hold hot tea. With a short delicate handle, a teacup has a large open top, and often tapers to the foot, creating a hemispherical shape. Teacups can come in ornate sets, either as part of a full china service, or as part of a tea-specific set, which would also include saucers, a sugar bowl, a creamer, and a teapot. A saucer (page 134) always sits below a teacup, preventing spills as well as keeping the heat from the cup from damaging the table.

TEAPOT

A teapot is a vessel made to brew and serve hot tea; it serves as the centerpiece of any tea set. Usually made from either porcelain or ceramic, though thin metal versions are also popular, especially in restaurants, teapots range in size from pots that produce a single serving to larger versions with multiple-person capacity. A teapot has a spout to pour from and a handle; the top of the pot is always lidded to trap the heat. First, hot water is added to the pot, then tea is introduced via tea bags, a tea infuser or ball (page 146), or a filter that specially fits into the opening on top. Some special models have a filter built into the spout, allowing for tea leaves to be added directly to the water. After the specified waiting time, brewed tea is then ready to be poured into a teacup (above) or mug (page 141) for drinking; tea that steeps too long with the leaves can become overly astringent.

TEA INFUSER

A tea infuser, also known as a tea ball, is a small mesh or perforated container that holds loose tea leaves as they steep in a cup or tea pot. A precursor to disposable teabags, the infuser is made out of metal or silicone and allows the drinker to steep the leaves as long as they like, then remove them to prevent excessive astringency. They are usually shaped like a basket or ball (with hinges that allow the infuser to open and close) but come in novelty designs as well. To make removal easier, they hook onto the rim of the cup or pot or are attached to a chain or long handle.

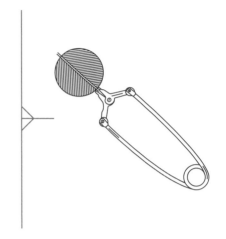

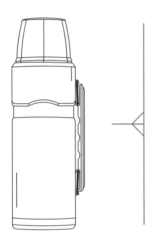

THERMOS

A thermos, also known as a vacuum flask, is an insulated food or beverage container, meant to keep food at its original temperature rather than equalizing with its environmental temperature. Most often used for hot or cold drinks, soups, and stews, a thermos consists of two flasks, one placed inside the other and sealed at the mouth, where the void between them has been partially emptied of air; this creates a near-vacuum, which allows for less heat conduction. Thermos is also a brand name for a popular vacuum flask company.

TUMBLER

A tumbler is a broad term for any glass or cup without a stem or handle, including an Old Fashioned glass (page 142), highball (page 140), or a shot glass (page 143). It can describe a variety of sizes and shapes, and can be made of glass or plastic. The word *tumbler* is confusing as most tumblers have flat bottoms, making them unlikely to tumble over; the etymology is unclear.

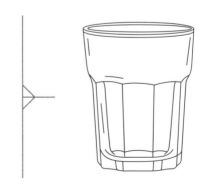

WINE GLASS

A wineglass is a specialized type of drinking glass used exclusively for drinking wine. Traditionally, wineglasses are stemmed glasses with a wide goblet-like bowl and a slightly tapered top; some contemporary designs feature classic bowl shapes, but forego a stem. Specific bowl size and shape vary depending on the varietal of grape in the wine and the tastes and smells one wants to emphasize; a wide glass makes for a larger surface area of wine, which means more alcohol evaporation. The tapering, or lack thereof, of the top of the glass captures or dissipates the aroma compounds and reduces or encourages evaporation. White-wine glasses tend to be smaller (for better temperature control) and are often more slender; red-wine glasses tend to be larger (allowing for an easier swirl, which aerates the wine) and wider (for more oxygen exposure). See champagne glass (page 138) for discussion on sparkling wines.

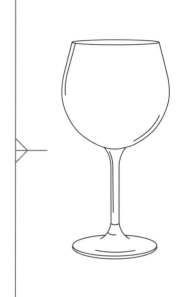

Wineglass Overload

There are many opinions regarding pairing a wine with its proper glass, and it can be both confusing and costly to keep up. While the style and shape of a glass can certainly affect the taste and smell of the wine held inside, not everyone has the capacity or interest to house a variety of glass types. In that case, there are so-called universal wineglasses, specially made to work well for a wide range of varietals.

Flatware

BOMBILLA

BUTTER KNIFE

CAKE SERVER

CHOPSTICKS

CHOPSTICK REST

DESSERT FORK

FORK

GRAPEFRUIT SPOON

LOBSTER/CRAB CRACKER

LOBSTER FORK/PICK

SALAD FORK

SOUP SPOON

SPOON

STEAK KNIFE

STRAW

SUJEO

TABLE KNIFE

TEASPOON

TABLESPOON

A set table can include nothing more than a set of chopsticks or a spoon, or it can be a very over-the-top affair, with multiple forks, spoons, knives, and specialty items. While the service is the same—to move food into one's mouth—the execution and variety depends mostly on how formal an occasion the meal is. While some of the more obscure items really do make eating easier, it is more often the case that a special piece of flatware was created more for pomp than function.

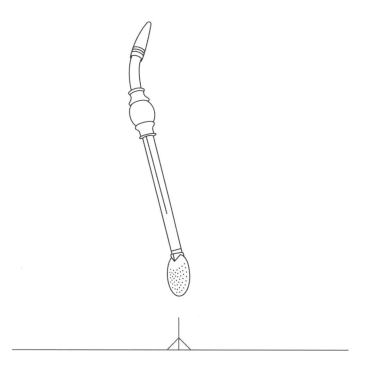

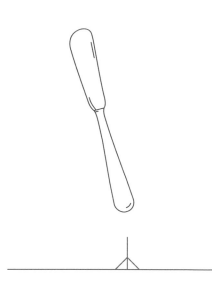

BOMBILLA

Bombilla is the Spanish word for a type of specialty straw used to drink mate, an unfiltered tea drink made of steeped yerba mate. In addition to being the national drink of Argentina and Uruguay, the beverage is popular in other parts of South America as well as in Syria and Lebanon. The design of a bombilla differs from the open-ended straw (page 158) and is particularly suited to mate, as the portion of the bombilla that sits in the traditional cup used to drink mate (often referred to as a gourd), is bulbous and perforated. These perforations allow sipped liquid to be easily filtered and separated from the leaves and stems of mate that are packed into a gourd, but which cannot travel through the bombilla's perforations. The bombilla is a necessary accompaniment to the drink, which otherwise would include sediment and particles not pleasant for consumption. Everyday versions of this straw are made of bamboo or reusable metal, such as stainless steel, copper, or nickel; specialty versions exist that are elaborately decorated with etchings and/or made of silver and gold.

BUTTER KNIFE

A butter knife is a small specialized table knife with a dull, nonserrated edge, appearing only at more formal occasions, and used exclusively for butter. There are two common varieties of the butter knife: a master butter knife and an individual butter knife. A master butter knife has a pointed tip that helps diners move pats of butter from a communal plate to their bread plate. An individual butter knife is given to each diner; not having a pointed end means the butter knife will not tear the bread when used to spread butter.

Utensils of Yore

In mid-nineteenth-century England, industry was thriving and the incomes of middle- and upper-class households were higher than ever. This increased level of financial comfort meant more people were able to spend money on nonessential creature comforts, and so sets of silver cutlery became one common way to part the upwardly mobile from their hard-earned money. Having a variety of utensils at each place setting—often including multiple forks, spoons, and knives—was an easy way to signal status, and to display to others the extent of your wealth. Following this logic, it should come as no surprise that there were increasingly specialized serving pieces forged for certain foods or circumstances that went well beyond what any typical diner of the day might have required.

Some of these newfangled pieces remain (relatively) popular, like the pickle fork, which is used exclusively for plucking a pickle out of a dish. A long-handled fork with two or three prongs, sometimes with notches in the tines so that the pickle won't fall off the fork in transport, a pickle fork is also referred to as a cocktail fork or an olive fork, and can be used for spearing all manner of edible garnishes. Fish forks and knives are always presented to diners as a set, and are smaller than dinner forks and knives. A fish knife has a broad blade that is helpful in lifting the fish to the fork; some versions also include a notch to help separate bones.

Other pieces which caught on in their day are a rarity now. A cake breaker is one example. With its comb-like vertical tines, this serving utensil is made for cutting neat slices of angel food cake, whose delicate crumb and airy interior might be crushed if a regular knife or cake server is used. Children also had their own diminutive, highly ornamented flatware, often consisting of small-handled spoons, loop-handled spoons, or "pushers," tiny handled hoes that aided the child in maneuvering their food onto a fork or spoon. Other unusual pieces included utensils for picking up toast (a large broad-based fork with wide tines), narrow scoopers for removing marrow from bones, "sporks" for eating ice cream, pierced or perforated flat spoons for picking up tomato slices (the holes drained the liquid away), and servers for various specific foods like oysters, potatoes, or bonbons. A trip to an antique shop will inevitably turn up some of these unusual and rare pieces.

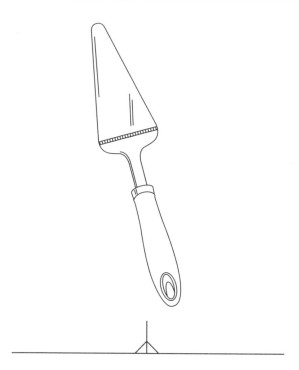

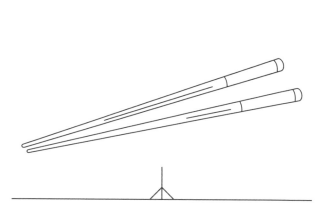

CAKE SERVER

A cake or pie server is a flat triangular-headed utensil used to cut and serve slices of cake or pie. Its shape mirrors the wedge shape of the piece of pie or cake cut from a whole, which means the section will be served intact and neat. The cake server itself is able to cut through softer desserts and savory quiches by using its edge, but sometimes a knife is also employed to cleanly cut each slice; in those cases, the server is used only for transferring each piece to an individual plate.

CHOPSTICKS

Originating in China thousands of years ago and later used throughout Japan, Korea, and Vietnam, among other countries, chopsticks are two thin sticks used for conveying food into your mouth with one hand. Food in countries that rely on chopsticks is often prepared in bite-size pieces for this reason; forks and knives are not commonly used (though spoons still appear). Chopsticks are typically tapered, and can be made from a wide variety of materials including wood, bamboo, porcelain, melamine, and metal. Confucius, with his nonviolent teachings, may have furthered the use of chopsticks in his time, as he famously stated that "the honorable and upright man . . . allows no knives on his table," thus encouraging other means for eating.

Chopstick Etiquette

There are many rules and customs when it comes to using chopsticks. One common offense is to stand one's chopsticks upright in a bowl of rice, which too closely recalls incense sticks at a funeral. Rubbing disposable chopsticks together to whittle away any splinters is also discouraged, although unknowing American eaters often do this with disposable break-apart chopsticks; it implies that one thinks the chopsticks are cheap, and can be insulting to the restaurant. When in doubt, follow the lead of a native user.

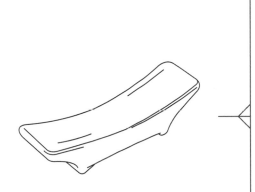

CHOPSTICK REST

Also called a spoon rest, the chopstick rest is a small piece of table setting meant to raise the eating end of a set of chopsticks (and/or spoon) off the table, like a pillow raises one's head off a mattress. Obviously, this tool is most popular in countries where chopsticks are common, like China, Japan, Vietnam, and the Koreas. Like a stovetop spoon rest (page 244), the purpose of this tabletop item is to keep the chopsticks or spoon sanitary for eating, as well as to prevent the table from becoming soiled by the utensils. While simple versions of a chopstick rest consist of little more than a small, baton-shaped piece of wood, designs and materials vary greatly. Rests are commonly made of wood, ceramic, enamel, stone, or metal, and often feature specialized decorations depicting animals or other whimsical forms. One design feature that almost all rests share is some kind of slightly raised sides or indentations in the middle that keeps the chopsticks from rolling off the rest. Restaurant patrons who are given paper-wrapped chopsticks can fashion their own rests by folding the wrapper into a disposable chopstick rest.

DESSERT FORK

Very similar to a salad fork (page 157), the dessert fork, also called a pastry or pie fork, has a shorter handle than a dinner fork and usually has four tines. The left tine is thicker than the others, so that diners can use the edge of the fork to cut through pastry, as a knife is not normally provided with dessert. The dessert fork often comes as part of a set of formal flatware, though it may also be packaged separately, along with dessert spoons. If necessary, a dessert fork can easily be replaced by a salad fork, especially if placed above the plate (at the 12 o'clock position), which is where any dessert cutlery is stationed unless it is brought directly to the table with the dessert.

FORK

The personal table fork, also sometimes called a dinner fork, is a utensil with tines that are used to bring food from one's plate to one's mouth. First used as a dining implement by seventh century Byzantine emperors and members of their royal court, table forks didn't become ubiquitous in western Europe and its former colonies until the middle of the nineteenth century, before which time it was standard practice to eat using nothing but one's hands and a knife. Early fork designs featured only two prongs, and were used primarily for spearing or stabbing food, but later versions evolved to include additional and slightly curved tines, which helped with scooping food. In a set of flatware, each table setting usually includes a salad or dessert fork as well as the dinner fork, the largest of the three, plus a knife, tablespoon, and teaspoon. Specialty forks were introduced during the Victorian era, including single-use forks such as a pickle fork, oyster fork, or cocktail fork.

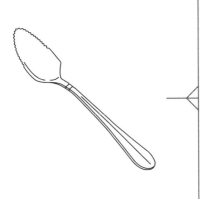

GRAPEFRUIT SPOON

In the same family as a grapefruit knife (page 230), a grapefruit spoon is a specialized spoon designed to help a diner in the eating of a halved grapefruit. The bowl of this spoon is slightly pointed to help make a smooth entry as it is inserted into each section of the fruit. In addition, the entire perimeter of the spoon's bowl is serrated, to aid in cutting each section of the fruit away from the peel as well as the interior membrane. The edges of the spoon are not so sharp as to threaten the diner's mouth; the spoon itself is used for cutting the sections of fruit as well as actually eating them.

A Casual Utensil

As opposed to most flatware, a spork (a combination of fork and spoon) is a specialized utensil not normally found in formal sets of cutlery. Nonetheless, in spite of its relative obscurity, the spork has been popular since the late nineteenth century. With its shallow, spoon-like bowl, shaped to scoop liquid or sauce, as well as its very short stubby tines cut into the end of the bowl in order to spear food, the spork is meant to accomplish the particular eating actions associated with both a fork and a spoon. Some detractors might say that the spork can really do neither. The bowl is very small and shallow, with little capacity for food, plus any scooping action is bound to be interrupted by the tines scraping against the edge of a bowl or cup and catching there. Also, the gripping or stabbing power of the diminutive tines is minimal, as they are really more similar to a serrated edge than a set of prongs. These days, the spork is usually a utility utensil, wielded for its efficiency, when both a fork and spoon are not practical or possible. For example, sporks are often the utensil given in school cafeterias and prisons; they can also be found at many campsites, or attached to a to-go container. Often disposable and made of plastic, wood, or bamboo, reusable sporks also exist and are typically fashioned from stainless steel, plastic, or aluminum.

LOBSTER/CRAB CRACKER

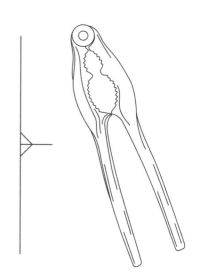

A lobster cracker, also known as a crab cracker, is a hinged, heavy-duty tool used to crack cooked lobsters and crabs at the table in order to access the meat inside. Like pliers, the two sides of the cracker open and you insert the shellfish, then are pressed together like a clamp with a single hand to exert force and break the shell. At its most basic, the two arms are straight and usually made of metal. More intricate versions have bluntly serrated teeth on the interior edge to better hold the shells, and can be shaped with a small indentation toward the hinge and a larger indentation below, meant to accommodate both smaller crabs and larger lobsters.

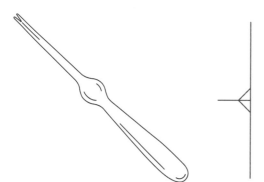

LOBSTER FORK/PICK

A lobster fork or pick is a specialized piece of flatware used at the table to help the eater carefully remove intact bits of meat from a lobster's claws and legs. The fork often has two straight sharp tines; the pick has a single point. These implements can also be used for extracting other delicate foods encased in a hard shell, like crab or crawfish.

Snailware

While a lobster pick is the perfect tool for extracting bits of lobster or crab meat from legs, claws, and other joints, creatures like snails have smaller shells that require tinier tools for the job. In France, escargot are often served in a very hot dish with individual indentations for each snail. In this case, a pair of specially made tongs are provided, which feature metal loops that fit around the curved outer shell of the snail. These tongs allow the diner to hold the hot shells while simultaneously employing a tiny snail fork to remove the meat. In Spain, snails are usually served more informally, in a bowl; toothpicks or even needles are provided to diners to fish out the snail from its shell.

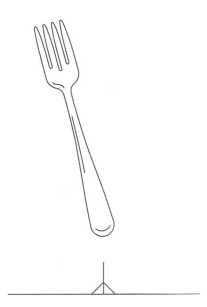

SALAD FORK

In addition to the most common dinner fork, the salad fork (also sometimes called or used as a dessert fork) is included in most sets of flatware. These special forks have shorter tines than a dinner fork, and the leftmost tine is often a bit fatter to aid in cutting through the crust of a pie or a vegetable as needed, as one traditionally doesn't often use a knife with salad or dessert.

SOUP SPOON

The soup spoon is a specialized utensil intended for consuming soup. The Western soup spoon, which first appeared in eighteenth century Europe, is usually made of some sort of metal, with a deeper, circular bowl than other table spoons, which is more conducive for holding liquid. The Chinese soup spoon is usually ceramic and shaped like a small ladle with a short handle pointed up at a 45-degree angle.

SPOON

The most commonplace of table utensils, the spoon is widely used in both Eastern and Western cultures, and consists of a long handle attached to a mouth-size concave bowl. A variety of specialized spoons are available in formal sets of flatware: soup spoon, dessert spoon, demitasse spoon, and serving spoon (page 242).

STEAK KNIFE

A steak knife is a very sharp table knife intended specifically for cutting a cooked steak, or other tough cut of meat, on an individual's plate. A steak knife's sharp blade is often made of stainless steel and is either serrated or smooth, and its handle can be made of wood, plastic, or metal, among other materials. Until World War II, most everyday table knives were sharp, but this required significant effort to keep the blades sharpened and polished. In upper class households, these tasks were accomplished by servants, who were becoming less common by the mid-twentieth century. Therefore, a need for a table knife requiring less upkeep emerged, and the surging popularity of steak knives in the 1950s pointed to the general public's only occasional desire for a sharp utensil at the table.

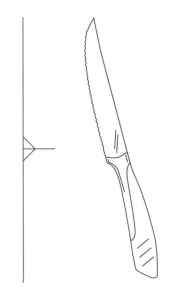

STRAW

A type of utensil, a straw is an individual, open-ended tube that is used to suck a liquid from a cup directly into one's mouth. The majority of straws are disposable plastic versions, included with drinks consumed at restaurants and bars. The size and shape of straws vary; short, skinny straws are commonly included with mixed alcoholic drinks (sometimes more than one), tall versions are given with water and soda at fast-food and casual restaurants, and wider types are provided for thicker drinks like milkshakes. Extra wide versions are made exclusively for bubble tea, so that the individual tapioca beads can be sucked through the straw into the drinker's mouth. Novelty straws might include various loops and accordioned sections that bend. The straw has come under fire recently as these single-use versions are not usually recyclable and therefore create excess waste. Straws made of metal, silicone, and even paper are becoming increasingly popular, allowing straw-using diehards to carry their own reusable versions.

Drinking Straws and Drunkenness

Straws are a common cocktail accompaniment in many bar settings, used for both drinking as well as spearing a garnish like olives or a cherry. Stories exist concerning drinking alcohol through a straw and how it can increase the drinker's level of drunkenness. While it's true that drinking an alcoholic beverage through a straw can increase the speed by which it is consumed, which could make one drunk faster, the use of the straw itself has no effect on the way alcohol affects the drinker. To avoid drunkenness, just drink less alcohol.

SUJEO

Sujeo is the word for the set of utensils used to eat Korean cuisine. A sujeo set includes both a spoon with a shallow round or oval bowl attached to a long, thin handle, and a set of chopsticks. Both the chopsticks and the spoon are made of the same material—often metal, such as stainless steel. The word *sujeo* is a hybrid of the individual Korean words for spoon, *sutgarak*, and chopsticks, *jeotgarak*. Traditionally, this set of utensils is used at the same time, though it is not considered polite to hold the spoon and the chopsticks together in the same hand. The chopsticks can be laid on the table at any time, but the spoon may be placed on the table only if it has not yet been used.

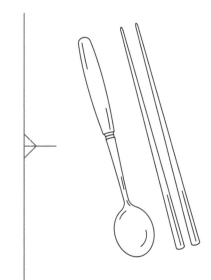

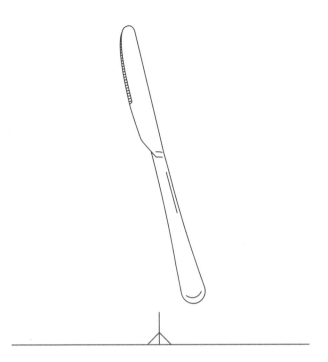

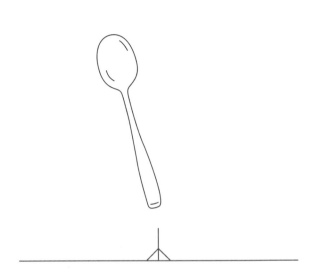

TABLE KNIFE

A table knife is perhaps the oldest table utensil: a sharpened edge used for cutting with a handle on one end. As food used to be prepared more often in cruder or larger pieces, a combination of one's hands and a knife were necessary to consume one's serving. Styles and customs regarding the table knife have changed over time, with the blade of the knife being pointed (to aid in stabbing a piece of food to bring to one's mouth) to blunted (popularized by King Louis XIV, who disliked when his companions picked their teeth with the point of their knives), to serrated, to sharp, to dull. Most contemporary table knives are not very sharp, nor serrated (see steak knife, page 158), as keeping a sharp edge requires additional maintenance. In many western civilizations, knives are still commonplace at the table; in many eastern civilizations, food is often prepared to be bite-size, thus eliminating the need for knives for each individual.

TEASPOON

A teaspoon is a small oval-head spoon used for individual stirring, sipping, or (possibly originally) adding sugar to tea or coffee. It is also commonly used as a primary utensil in a simple place setting along with a dinner fork (page 81) and table knife (opposite), though sometimes a tablespoon (opposite page) is preferred. In addition, a teaspoon is also a unit of measure, equal to 5 milliliters or ⅓ of a tablespoon. In recipes, the teaspoon is often abbreviated as a lowercase "t." The flatware version of a teaspoon is less official than the measuring type of teaspoon and should not be used as a standard, but it should still hold approximately the same amount.

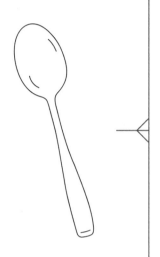

TABLESPOON

A tablespoon is a small, wide spoon with a shallow oval bowl made for individual use. Along with its smaller cousin, the teaspoon (opposite page), the tablespoon is one of two spoons included in most standard sets of flatware. If no soup spoon is available, a tablespoon may be used as a substitute as it is large enough to provide a hearty mouthful when eating soups and stews. The tablespoon is also a unit of measuring volume and contains a little less than 15 milliliters—it is equal to 3 teaspoons. In recipes, a tablespoon measurement is often abbreviated as an uppercase "T." Like the flatware teaspoon, the official capacity of a flatware tablespoon should not be relied on if exactness is what's needed, though it should hold the same approximate amount as its more precisely calibrated measuring spoon counterpart.

Flatware Strategies

A large assortment of flatware at a place setting can be confusing to the diner if they are not familiar with that level of formality. In short, the rule about which piece of flatware to use when is to start with the piece on the outside of the setting, located furthest from the plate, and then to move inward as courses progress. Dessert utensils are often put horizontally at the top of the plate, and bread service utensils will be located by the bread plate.

Serveware on the Go

BENTO BOX

LUNCH BOX

PICNIC BASKET

TIFFIN

Serveware is not just the surfaces or dishes one eats from at the table, but also the pieces that make it possible to take prepared food outside of the home. Most cultures have ways to transport cooked food, whether to bring it to work or school, or to a more frivolous function like a picnic.

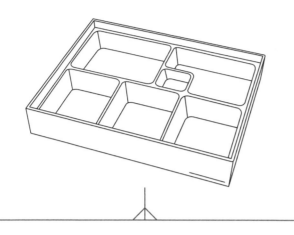

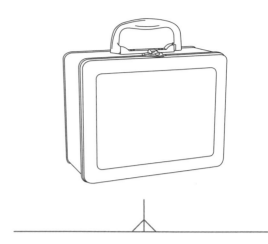

BENTO BOX

A Japanese creation, the bento box is a vessel made for eating a single serving of prepared food, often a midday meal. The box itself can refer to a container with a tight-fitting lid, designed to transport food from the home to the workplace, for example, or can refer to a single open-topped vessel, commonly used in restaurants. Either way, most bento box designs are somewhat elaborate, with various interior compartments and sections to keep different foods separated. This feature is what differentiates the bento box most from other forms of lunch boxes (opposite and page 167). The multiple compartments can be filled with a wide variety of fish, meat, rice, vegetables, and pickles, often making a well-balanced and nutritious meal. The presentation of the food inside a bento box is often part of the experience. *Oekakiben* is a Japanese word that is often translated as "picture bento," which refers to the fact that this type of bento has food created in the style and shape of people, animals, scenes, and more; *kyaraben* is another type of bento in which the food is presented in the form of popular anime or comic book characters. Bento boxes can be made of a variety of materials, from disposable plastic and paper versions (sold at convenience stores and train stations) to reusable lacquerware, tin, plastic, or metal options.

LUNCH BOX

A lunch box is a closed vessel designed to contain and carry prepared food. Originating as a way to transport food when there was no time to return home for a meal, a lunchbox in the nineteenth century came in the form of a simple pail with a lid, meant to keep a child's or working person's midday meal from being damaged or polluted while at school or work. By the twentieth century, lunch boxes began to be manufactured as uniform, rectangular, hard-sided containers with a lid that latched shut and a handle for easy carrying. Made of plastic, vinyl, or metal, these lunch boxes sometimes contained a specially fitted thermos (page 146), which allowed the carrier to transport hot or cold food and beverages. Lunch box decorations range from basket motifs (echoing a picnic basket, opposite page) to the most popular icons of the day—from cartoon characters to bands and movie stars. Contemporary versions of lunch boxes have changed shape again, and now come as soft-sided insulated bags; some of which can be frozen to help keep food cold.

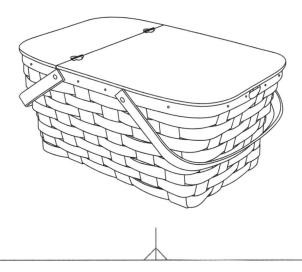

PICNIC BASKET

A picnic basket is a large container that holds the contents of a picnic and makes them easily transportable. Quintessentially, a picnic basket is made of woven wicker and opens at the top, with two hinged flaps and handles. Modern day versions are also made of wood, bamboo, plastic, or insulated fabrics, which have the added benefit of keeping the contents cold. Picnic baskets now have various designs that are not always top-opening, and some options come with loops and holders attached to the outside for bottles, and sometimes even have straps that allow carrying the basket like a backpack. Though included contents often vary, some picnic baskets are merely empty containers for holding food and drinks, and perhaps one's own cutlery and serveware, as necessary. More extravagant baskets come already stocked with their own china (often plastic, for durability and lighter weight), wine and/or water glasses, flatware, napkins, and a blanket. These more elaborate setups might also include a bottle opener (page 188), corkscrew (page 190), sharp knife, cutting board for cheese and fruit, and even a small set of salt and pepper shakers (page 133). The more opulent versions are often carefully designed, with straps and holders to keep all of the included pieces in place and out of the way, so that there is still room for food and drinks.

Picnic Preparedness

A picnic, where people eat in a park, field, forest, or garden, has the potential to be an idyllic outdoor experience. When properly supplied with special foods to share, and cold (or hot!) drinks to sip, a picnic should be relaxing and fulfilling, both psychologically as well as culinarily. But, like most outdoor experiences—camping, going to the beach, hiking—being well prepared has a big impact.

First, make sure to be well supplied, even if it requires a wagon and/or a backpack to transport items. The picnic mantra should always be "more is more," ensuring everyone is well fed and cared for. Extra wine has a way of getting drunk, and a few more frozen water bottles will keep drinks cold. If the picnic is a success, picnickers will be grazing for hours. A sharp knife and cutting board aren't absolutely necessary for slicing fruit, but they sure are better than attempting to cut with a dull knife on a paper plate.

Second, remember the elements. Shade is key for comfort, so pick the location carefully. Good weather is a must; if the forecast calls for rain, change the date. Make sure to pack extra blankets—providing more places to sit as well as possible layers for changes of temperature. Bug spray and sunscreen will ward off troublesome ailments. And, of course, bring food that will not only survive at room temperature for the whole day, but will be improved by it: think pain bagnat (the nicoise sandwich of tuna, capers, and tomatoes), cheese, and charcuterie, not ice cream bars or anything containing dairy or mayonnaise.

Third, go all out. Picnics are all about leisure and fun. Make a playlist especially for the event. Pack Bananagrams, a frisbee, bocce balls, or even the crossword for a fun activity. And most of all, bring foods that classify as treats and goodies—this is not a time for moderation or calorie counting!

TIFFIN

A tiffin is a type of lunch box (page 164) popular in India, Singapore, Malaysia, and Indonesia, among other parts of Asia. Also called a *dabbas* or a *rantang*, among other country-specific names, a tiffin consists of multiple stacked containers with a single tight-fitting lid and clips that hold the set together; they are often made of tin, steel, aluminum, or plastic. Similar to a bento box (page 164), one of the defining features of a tiffin is its ability to hold more than one dish at a time; often the bottom layer of the stack is reserved for rice, while upper levels hold stews and curries.

Tiffin Transport

In Mumbai, tiffins are so vital to the community and culture of the city that an entire job force was created just to transport them to individual workers throughout the city every day, guaranteeing a hot lunch onsite. Known as dabbawalas, these delivery people travel primarily on bicycles and trains. The process of collecting and distributing these boxes begins either at home or at a restaurant; from there, dabbawalas pick up the tiffins and deliver them to specific locations by a specific time. Though simple enough in theory, this delivery process represents a huge and incredibly complicated logistical system. So successful is the process of the dabbawalas that they have been formally studied for efficiency and on-time distribution.

Serving Dishes

These dishes run the range from simple and functional—a communal vessel from which people serve large quantities of food—to highly ornate pieces sold with sets of china. Of the serving dishes, unless you live in a more formal household, platters and trays will be used most often, while more obscure items like a gravy boat might appear only at large social events.

BUTTER DISH

A butter dish is a simple container for serving butter; it can be made from metal, ceramic, or plastic. Butter dishes can be communal pots that are packed with butter; or individual tiny dishes situated with the bread-and-butter plate (page 128).

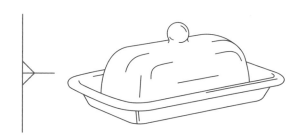

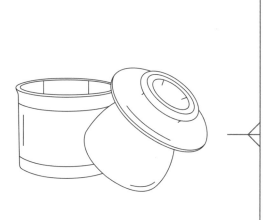

BUTTER KEEPER

Also known as a French butter dish, a butter keeper is used to keep butter fresh without refrigeration. The butter keeper has two parts: the bottom, a ceramic straight sided jar, and the top, a ceramic lid that when lifted reveals a bell-shaped bowl suspended from the underside. The butter is stored in the bell-shaped bowl and the base of the keeper is filled with water. When the lid is on the butter keeper, the butter is suspended upside down, and the exposed area of butter is submerged in the water. This keeps the butter airtight and cool, which keeps it fresh even at room temperature. This is appealing to those who do not want to refrigerate their butter, keeping it soft and spreadable without spoilage.

CAKE STAND

A cake stand is a raised plate or platter used for presenting and serving cakes. The platform, which can vary in size and shape, sits upon a leg or legs which holds the cake at higher-than-table level. Often made of ceramic, metal, or plastic, a cake stand can be decorative and formal or simple and casual, depending on the context, but is meant to show off the decorated confection on a table of other foods, hence its height. Some cake stands include a cover, which is high and wide enough to not nick the cake and ruin its ornamentation.

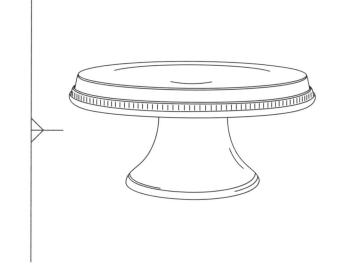

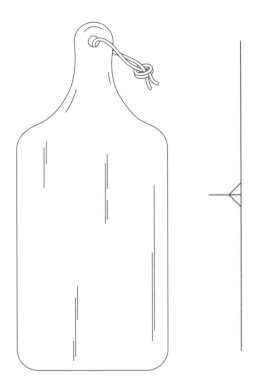

CHEESEBOARD

A cheeseboard is a flat surface made specifically for serving a variety of cheeses and accouterments. If one cut cheese on a porcelain plate or platter, the surface could be scratched. As its name implies, cheeseboards are frequently constructed from hardwood, though stone (for example, slate or marble) has become an increasingly popular alternative. Plastic and glass are also available; soft wood should be avoided as it absorbs smells. In addition to adding a certain panache to a cheese selection, a cheeseboard is most useful as a strong and sturdy cutting surface—necessary as the cheese is presented in large pieces that the individual serves themselves (often using a cheese knife, page 228).

Cheeseboard Extras

In addition to a set of cheese knives, many items can take a cheeseboard from basic to extravagant. Identifying the cheeses is a worthwhile task, especially if time and money has been spent acquiring them: use specially made signs, which you can make using a washable marker and post into each cheese block, or scribble directly onto slate using chalk. While the cheese is the main event, pairings with other foods can highlight different tastes and textures and make for a beautiful presentation. Try fresh fruit (peeled and sliced as necessary), dried fruit, nuts, olives, preserved meats (salami, coppa, Serrano ham, etc.), honey, chutneys, jams (fig, onion, etc.), and crackers or bread. Group single ingredients together to keep the board from getting cluttered, and place them near the best cheese pairing. But feel no pressure—a simple glass of wine on the side might be the best extra of all.

GRAVY BOAT

Usually made either of porcelain or a metal such as stainless steel or silver, a gravy boat is a vessel for serving gravy or any other sauce. It holds enough liquid for several servings, and is passed at the table so guests can serve themselves. Much like a short and stout jug or a teapot without a lid, a gravy boat has a handle on one end and spout to pour from on the other. Designs vary; as such, some gravy boats are freestanding containers, others are physically attached to a plate to catch drips, and others are highly ornate versions with feet on the bottom to keep the boat from touching the table.

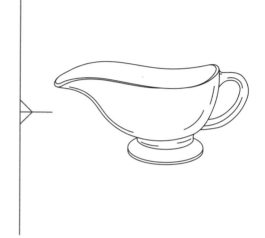

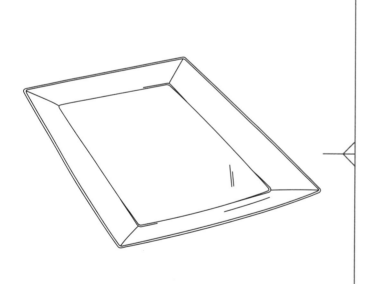

PLATTER

A platter is a large, flat plate, available in a variety of shapes, used to present food to a group for serving. Since platters are inherently made for presentation, they are sometimes ornate and included in sets of china, where they are often the grandest and most expensive piece in the set, or made from other valuable materials like silver or gold plate. Other platters are made from more modest metal, glass, wood, and plastic, and operate simply as a vessel from which people serve themselves food. Platters occasionally come with handles, which makes maneuvering the heavy piece and its accompanying food easier.

SALAD BOWL

A salad bowl is a large serving dish made specifically for preparing and presenting salads. Often made of wood, glass, or ceramic, a salad bowl needs to be wide and tall enough to contain multiple vegetables, including voluminous leafy greens like lettuce, and to allow the components to be tossed thoroughly with a salad dressing or vinaigrette without sending any ingredients tumbling over the side. Matching individually-size salad bowls are sometimes merchandised with the larger serving bowl.

TRAY

A tray is used for moving, serving, or presenting food, often multiple dishes at once. It can be decorative, like special silver or porcelain pieces, or simple and practical, like an individual plastic tray at a cafeteria, or a metal tray used by a waiter to shuttle a round of drinks from the bar. Depending on its material, it also can function as a serving platter for food that is very large, like a whole fish or a ornate pastry, or when a larger surface is needed, like a cheese plate for a crowd.

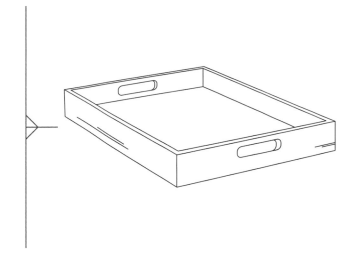

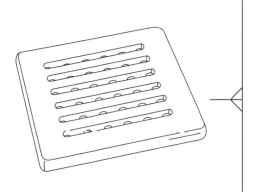

TRIVET

A trivet is a protective stand made of wood, glass, metal, cork, or ceramic—anything that is relatively heatproof. Often ornate in design, trivets form a thin physical barrier between a container of hot, wet, or cold food and drink and a surface, thereby preventing the dish from marring the surface on which it sits. In purpose, a trivet is similar to a coaster (page 138), but larger. Fancier versions have feet to further prevent heat transfer, but most are merely a flat surface upon which a dish or pan is placed.

UTENSILS
& GADGETS

Baking & Decorating Tools

Baking requires its own set of specialized tools for prep, for cooking, and for decorating. Note that some of these utensils have applications in the savory kitchen as well.

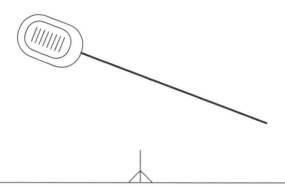

CAKE TESTER

A cake tester is a thin, needle-shaped rod, usually 2 to 4 inches long, with a tiny tab handle at one end for holding between one's fingers. Per its name, the cake tester is meant to test cakes for doneness. To use, one simply inserts the nontabbed end of the tester into a baked cake to measure how wet or dry its interior is, therefore determining if it needs additional time in the oven. In general, if a tester is inserted into a cake and comes out clean, without any attendant crumbs or juices, the cake is done baking. In addition to its namesake task, a cake tester can be used for testing the doneness of other foods as well. This tool's rigidity gives the user a good read on the resistance of the interior of whatever food it is poked into; fish is a popular subject for testing this way. In addition to testing the consistency of the inside of a food, the cake tester can also be a rudimentary indicator of temperature; because the rod is made of heavy gauge wire, it conducts heat well. By inserting the rod into a food and then gently pressing it onto one's lip or chin (a heat sensitive zone), one can broadly surmise whether the inside of a food is cold, warm, or hot, which can indicate doneness. Finally, the cake tester's slim profile (as opposed to a fork or a paring knife) will not disturb the presentation of the outside of any food, nor will it create a hole large enough to drain any internal juices, making it both a subtle and effective tool for judgment.

Checking Doneness

Seasoned cooks know that one cannot trust the time indication given in the cooking directions of a recipe—like the instruction to "bake for 15 minutes," for example—except for general planning purposes. The individual calibration of stovetops and ovens can vary widely from home to home. The seasonality, quality, and age of the ingredients can affect how long it takes to cook them. Even the altitude can affect the time needed for cooking, among many other considerations.

Luckily, well-written recipes will give other indications of doneness in addition to a time marker: clues like "until bright green and crisp-tender" and "until reduced and glossy" are all helpful visual and physical indications a cook can use to deduce whether the food is at the stage it should be. In addition to this information, there are tools that one can use to help judge for doneness. A meat thermometer (page 110) or a candy thermometer (page 108) can indicate the exact internal temperature of a food, which makes determining the doneness of many foods a cinch.

Texture is another facet of doneness. The phrase "fork-tender" represents this notion, but linguistically and practically, it is not as fine-tuned as it could be, as a fork (page 154) is a relatively blunt utensil: if something is prodded with a fork and is deemed tender, it may well be overdone. Similarly, a paring knife (page 233), another popular tester, is so sharp that it will puncture even raw food easily, so should not be seen as a reliable gauge of tenderness. A cake tester (opposite page) is a better tool for appraising internal texture. Thinner than a fork's tine and less sharp than a knife, the cake tester can be inserted into a piece of meat or a fillet of fish (or a cake, obviously), and it will provide more information to the cook than most other utensils, regarding temperature and resistance, and it can do all of this without creating unsightly marks on the outside of the food. No matter your tool, interpreting this information takes practice, but it is truly the only way to tell if something is "done."

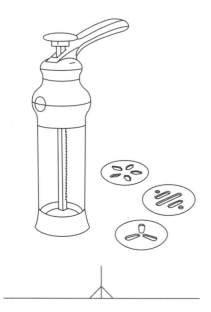

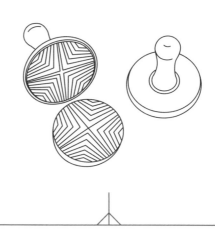

COOKIE PRESS

Constructed from a cylinder and a plunger, a cookie press extrudes cookie dough through various perforated plates to make a variety of designs. Most presses have a lever or trigger attached to the plunger that helps in making uniformly sized cookies. To use, press the end of the cylinder with the plate directly onto your cookie sheet and squeeze the trigger to push the dough through the disk, where it sticks to the sheet; then carefully remove the press from the cookie sheet. One note of caution: a cookie press is best used in conjunction with a fairly simple dough (like sugar cookie dough), and should not include any mix-ins, as they will not necessarily fit through the perforations in the disks.

COOKIE STAMP

Made of cast iron (or other metal), plastic, or wood, cookie stamps are hand-held etched blocks used to imprint a design onto the top of a piece of cookie dough prior to baking. Emblazoned with words, geometric designs, pictures of characters, and other decorative motifs, a cookie stamp is an easy way to add flair to plain cookies without needing to engage in more time- and skill-intensive decoration. Cookie stamps work by pressing the etched plate onto each circle of dough (ideally the dough has already been placed on a cookie sheet) and baking as directed. The final cookie should keep the imprint of the stamp's design, especially if the dough was kept cold prior to baking. Another type of cookie stamp is a stamp cut out—also known as a cookie cutter—which one presses upon a thin sheet of rolled out cookie dough. Once stamped, remove the excess dough from around the newly formed cookies so all that remains are the die-cut shapes of dough (in the shape of leaves, birds, or fir trees, for example). Before baking, reroll the scraps of dough into a new, thin sheet and stamp again to form even more cookies. To keep the dough from sticking to the stamp, coat the stamp with grease or flour. You may also choose to chill the stamp before using. All of these methods help keep the dough on the cookie sheet (page 58) instead of stuck to the stamp itself.

A Biscuit Press?

A cookie press is sometimes called a biscuit press, but do not make the mistake of trying to make American-style biscuits in it. If you do, the dough will become overworked and the sizes will be much too small for even a bite-size biscuit. The confusion stems from the fact that outside of the US, cookies are called biscuits. In short, the only biscuits one should make in this type of press are the sweet, sugar dough type (what Americans call cookies), best served with a cup of English tea.

DECORATING COMB

A decorating comb—also called a cake comb, cake scraper, or icing smoother—is a tool used for manipulating frosting or icing on a cake in order to add a flourish or finish to the final confection. While at-home bakers may find a need for this tool, a decorating comb is most commonly used by professional pastry chefs. One popular design of the comb consists of a rigid piece of triangular or rectangular plastic or metal with a variety of flat, jagged, or serrated edges. A comb or scraper can also feature a singular decorative edge attached to a handle. To use, one often first frosts the cake using a straight spatula (page 254) or offset spatula; after that, one applies the edge of a decorating comb to the smooth frosting by sweeping it with one's hand or while spinning the cake on a cake turntable (page 98) and keeping the comb still, creating a ridged or ribbed effect in the surface of the frosting. Some cake scrapers look very similar to a bench scraper, and can be used to frost a cake with a smooth finish; similarly, the flat edge of a multisided decorating comb can make a flat surface. Some other cake scrapers include a 90° angle (and are adjustable height-wise), so one can smooth or decorate the sides and the top of the cake at the same time.

PASTRY BAG

A pastry bag, also called a piping bag, is a cone-shaped vessel which is filled with loose-textured food (like batter, frosting, or icing) and then piped out of the tip by squeezing the large end of the bag with your hand. Made of canvas, cotton, various types of plastic, or other flexible materials, pastry bags are often used for extruding identically sized and shaped amounts of batter, like for cream puffs or meringues, or for filling pastries and donuts, or applying icing or frosting. A pastry bag can be fitted with a variety of pastry bag tips (opposite page), making the style and shape of the piping line anything from utilitarian to fine and decorative, depending on your visual intention. In addition to baking, pastry bags can be helpful for piping other soft foods, like devilled egg filling into egg whites. Pastry bags also come in disposable plastic versions, as they can be difficult to clean.

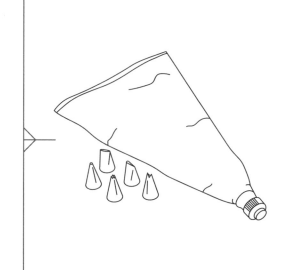

DIY Pastry Bags

In a pinch, a simple zip-top bag makes a reasonable substitute for a formal pastry bag. Just fill the bag as you would a pastry bag, then trim off one lower corner of the bag. You can either squeeze out the contents directly, or fit the hole with a pastry bag tip (opposite page). More exacting jobs can also be completed using a hand-spun cone of parchment paper with the tip cut off, which is a very good option for lettering decoration on cakes or cookies.

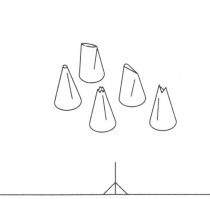

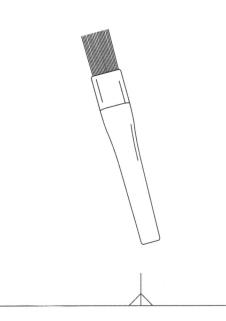

PASTRY BAG TIPS

Pastry bag tips are the metal or plastic decorative nozzles that are inserted into the hole at the end of a pastry bag (opposite page), and through which batter, icing, or frosting is extruded. Pastry tips come in a variety of styles and shapes (with standardized identifying numbers) that have different visual results when used. The most popular types include round tips for more utilitarian jobs and for writing, and star or shell tips that give a more ridged decorative result. More exotic types include tips specially made to create various flowers or leaves.

PASTRY BRUSH

A pastry brush, also known as a basting brush, is a small brush with boar, plastic, nylon, or silicone bristles used to apply a thin layer of an ingredient, often a fat, onto the surface of food that is cooking. For example, in baking, it is helpful for spreading an egg wash onto the surface of a pastry prior to baking, or applying melted butter in a thin layer onto filo sheets to be stacked for baklava. It can also be used for cake and cookie decoration. In cooking, basting brushes baste, meaning they are dipped in rendered cooking juices and reapplied to the food to help brown the outside of the food, such as when roasting a chicken. Basting brushes can also be helpful to apply a glaze onto food toward the end of cooking; the brush is best for achieving a thin layer with complete coverage.

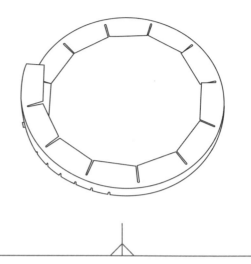

PIE BIRD

A pie bird—also known as a pie vent, pie chimney, pie whistle, or pie funnel—is an old-fashioned hollow ceramic or stoneware statuette formed in the shape of an open-beaked bird. The open beak creates a vent in the top crust of a pie, which makes this tool useful for releasing steam and, therefore, keeping the pastry crisp. To use, you sit the bird on the parcooked bottom crust, pour the filling around it, cover the pie with a vented top crust, allowing the birds head to poke through the vent, and then bake per usual. The steam inside the pie will funnel out through the bird's mouth, preventing steam inside the pie from building up and the filling from bubbling over. An alternative to using a pie bird would be simply cutting vents in the top crust of the pie, but this is decidedly less cute.

PIE CRUST SHIELD

Made of aluminum or lightweight silicone, a pie crust shield is a circular band of protection one places on an uncooked pie edge for the first few minutes of baking. When the pie has approximately 15 minutes left of cooking, the shield is then removed so that the crust can brown appropriately. If one does not have access to a pie crust shield and the crust is browning too fast, a homemade shield can be fashioned from tinfoil.

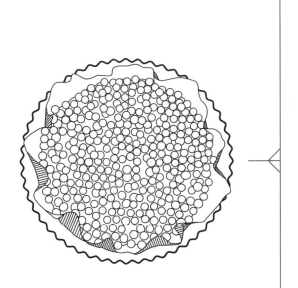

PIE WEIGHTS

When making a pie with either an uncooked filling like a mousse, or an especially wet filling that would impede the bottom crust from cooking through, many recipes will encourage bakers to "blind bake" their crust. During this first pre-bake, pie weights are placed onto the raw bottom pie crust to weigh down the dough so it doesn't puff up during cooking. Typically made of inedible ceramic or metal beads, pie weights also help keep the pie's intended shape by holding the sides of the dough to the edge of the pie plate (page 61), which otherwise might slump or shrink. Fifteen minutes is usually sufficient time for a blind bake, as the crust will continue cooking after the filling is added. Be sure to line your dough with a piece of foil or parchment paper before adding the weights; this will keep the weights clean and make it easy to remove them when you're ready to add your filling.

Beans to the Rescue

If you do not have pie weights, or if you're looking for a lower cost alternative, dried beans are a popular replacement for blind baking a pie crust. Beans can be used and reused in the same way as pie weights: to weight down the crust of a pie. However, once beans have been used in this manner, they should not be reconstituted and eaten.

Bar Tools

BOTTLE OPENER

COCKTAIL PICK

COCKTAIL SHAKER

COCKTAIL STRAINER

CORKSCREW

ICE CRUSHER

ICE TONGS

JIGGER

JULEP SPOON

MIXING GLASS

MUDDLER

A well-stocked bar should include a small set of tools to help create cocktails. Something as simple as a martini still requires a jigger, tongs, and a strainer, whether one likes it shaken or stirred, straight up or on the rocks. More complicated concoctions might require special tools to macerate fruits, crush herbs, or dissolve sugar.

BOTTLE OPENER

This handheld tool removes the caps of bottles
through the use of leverage. Designs vary widely,
but the concept is the same: the head of a bottle opener
is pressed down onto the top of a bottle cap, then, as
one creates an upward tilting motion with the handle
of the bottle opener, a discrete hook or edge on the
head of the opener is forced underneath the pleated lip
of the cap, prying it up and off. Very simple versions
are included in Swiss Army knives and corkscrews.

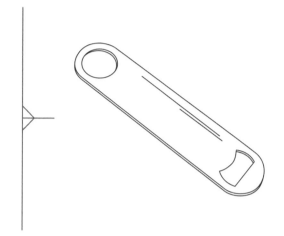

COCKTAIL PICK

A cocktail pick is a small wooden or metal skewer a few inches
long that is meant to hold a drink's special accouterment, such
as an olive, brandied cherry, or pickled onion. It has one sharp
end used to spear the ingredient, and the pick is long enough
to retrieve the ingredient if at some point during the drink's
consumption the drinker would like a nibble. Cocktail picks
either balance on the rim of the glass or rest in the drink itself,
allowing the skewered garnish to provide additional flavor. The
shape of a cocktail pick can be simple: such as a round, wooden
toothpick; or complex: such as a tiny, crepe-paper umbrella or a
plastic spear with a novelty top shaped like a mermaid. Like a
toothpick (page 269), a cocktail pick can also be used to skewer
small appetizers for a special presentation.

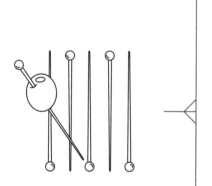

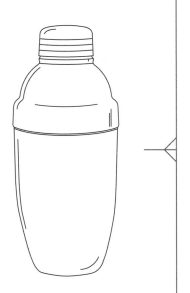

COCKTAIL SHAKER

A light, metal vessel meant for prepping and shaking cocktails, the cocktail shaker is a must-have in any at-home bartender's kitchen. The cocktail shaker has tall sloping sides, and the top has a fitted lid with an opening to pour from (sometimes with a mesh or perforated strainer built in) and a small cap to place over the opening to completely seal the shaker. To use, add ingredients and ice to the cup, put on the lid and the cap, and shake the entire container up and down; by agitating the liquids with the ice, the liquids are quickly chilled, and the ice melts a bit, deliberately diluting the drink by a small fraction. To serve, remove the cap and pour the drink through the opening into the glass of choice, leaving the ice behind in the shaker. The durability of the shaker is significant when making muddled drinks, as it allows the ingredients to be muddled directly in the vessel.

A Bartender's Shortcut

In a busy bar, lids, caps, and even strainers can feel fussy and may add unnecessary time to the mixing of a drink; plus these tools are more difficult to clean and can get lost in the sink. However, a mixing glass and the canister of a cocktail shaker are easy to clean—so often they are combined for a hybrid cocktail shaker. Ingredients and ice are added to the mixing glass (page 192), and the metal canister of the cocktail shaker is used as a lid by inverting it over the glass and tapping down to seal it before shaking. To break the seal, a bartender will knock the glass and canister against the bar top, and then strain the final drink into a glass using the rim of the shaker as a partial dam. No extraneous equipment needed.

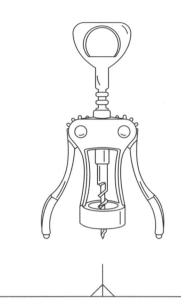

COCKTAIL STRAINER

After adding a drink's ingredients to a vessel and mixing them together, one uses a cocktail strainer—a perforated circular stainless-steel lid meant to strain out the ice and any large particles from the finished drink—to neatly pour the contents into the chosen serving glass. The Hawthorne strainer, the most common type of cocktail strainer, includes a metal spring fixed around the rounded edge, so that the strainer can sit snugly inside the lip of any mixing vessel and can easily be held in place by its short handle, even when inverted single handedly for pouring. A julep strainer is another subtype that consists of only a metal circle perforated by holes, with a long handle—this is meant to hold back the mint and other large particles of a julep from remaining in the final drink. A julep strainer can be used for drinks other than juleps, but note that the Hawthorne strains faster and more efficiently, making it the better tool for general use.

CORKSCREW

A corkscrew, also called a wine opener or wine key, is used to remove the cork from the neck of a wine bottle. Designs vary, but at its most basic, a corkscrew includes a metal spiral with a sharp point and a handle to rotate the spiral or screw into the cork. One then uses the handle to pull the spiral out of the bottle neck with the cork still attached. Most versions also include a lever of some sort to aid in pulling the spiral out. A popular style comes with a gear that raises handles on either side of the screw as it is driven into the cork; one can then press down the handles to pull the screw, with the cork, up and out of the bottle.

Obliterating Corkscrews?

Screw top closures for wine bottles, instead of cork stoppers, have been in existence since the 1950s, but the stigma remains about their use implying a wine is inexpensive or of low quality. There are many advantages of screw top closures, however. In addition to the convenience of not needing a corkscrew, a screw top is also better at resealing an opened bottle and avoids "cork taint," an affliction affecting up to one in every twelve bottles of wine, where musty-tasting TCA, a chemical compound, is found in the wine (this stems from a naturally occurring fungi in the cork reacting with another compound used to sterilize bottles). Will the romance of a cork, and by association, a corkscrew, eventually disappear? Only time will tell.

ICE CRUSHER

An ice crusher is a manual or electric gadget made for transforming large blocks or cubes of ice into smaller pieces. Most crushers allow for their users to select from a range of textures varying from coarse to fine. Manual versions require a crank to turn the internal blades, and can be difficult to use; electric versions are easier to handle and thus more popular.

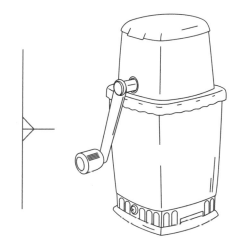

ICE TONGS

Ice tongs are a sanitary way to add ice to a cocktail shaker or a serving glass, and since most cocktails are served cold and hard alcohol is usually kept at room temperature, ice is a necessary ingredient for almost all mixed drinks. Bartenders know never to use a glass to retrieve ice out of the machine, as the rim can chip and contaminate the entire batch with its dangerous shards; using ice tongs or a scoop (page 241) is the only safe method of moving ice.

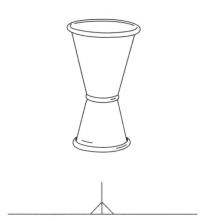

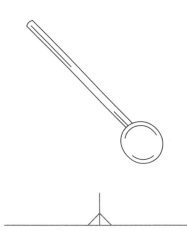

JIGGER

A jigger is a bartender's measuring device used to control how many shots of alcohol and other mixers will be included in each drink. Designs vary, but it is often cone-shaped and comes with a handle for ease of use. A single jigger consists of one vessel that holds a single 1½-ounce shot; a double jigger has two vessels in the shape of an hourglass, which hold two different amounts.

JULEP SPOON

A julep spoon is a tall spoon served with a mint julep where the handle of the spoon also encompasses a straw. This very specialized implement is helpful for drinks that contain crushed ice, like a julep, which can make drinking directly from the glass difficult and messy. The straw pulls the drink up from the bottom, making it easier to sip, and the spoon can be used to stir and break up clumps of ice.

MIXING GLASS

A sibling to the cocktail shaker, the mixing glass is used to mix and chill cocktails. Sometimes it is printed with popular cocktail recipes and demarcations indicating proper measurements for each ingredient. Most mixing glasses come with a simple metal top which can strain and pour. To use a mixing glass, one adds the liquor(s), mixers, and ice, stirs with a long spoon for about 15 to 20 seconds, and strains the cocktail through the accompanying metal top into a glass. If no metal top is provided, a cocktail strainer may be used.

Professional Bar Utensils

There is a plethora of additional bar utensils, but most are better suited for professional situations. Channel knives cut a groove of citrus zest, used for garnish. Fine sieves are employed to create the clearest, smoothest shaken drinks. Bar spoons are usually used merely to stir, a job that can be accomplished with any spoon, but their spiraled handle is sometimes used to make layered drinks, where the nozzle of a pourer on a bartender's handle of liquor can be applied to the spiral to dribble a layer of alcohol to float on top of a drink. These tools all add flair and polish to cocktails in a bar or restaurant setting, but are unlikely to find as much use in a home environment.

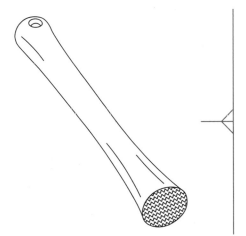

MUDDLER

Similar to—but longer than—a pestle, a muddler is a sturdy wooden or metal utensil with a blunt end used to smash fruit, herbs, or other cocktail ingredients in a shaker or glass, releasing their oils and juices. The end used to pound can have either a smooth or a textured surface, and which type one chooses will depend on the delicacy of your ingredients. To make a mojito, for example, one uses a textured muddler to macerate the limes, dissolve the sugar, and bruise the mint before adding the requisite ice, rum, and soda water to finish.

Crackers, Manipulators & Mashers

The kitchen is full of tools that help to change the form of food. These special implements press, crush, and otherwise break down foods.

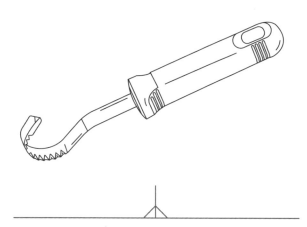

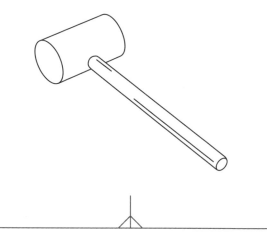

BUTTER CURLER

A butter curler is a tool that makes decorative pieces of butter for serving. Most commonly it takes the shape of a large hook with a serrated edge, but also can take the form of a slotted implement, similar to a cheese knife (page 228). Either way, when the butter is cool and the curler is warmed (by running under hot water and drying, for example), the butter curler can be dragged across the surface of the butter block, shaving off a thin piece that curls onto itself; the tool's serrations make the surface of the curl ridged. A butter curler works for chocolate as well.

CRAB HAMMER

Like a crab cracker (page 156), a crab hammer, usually made of wood, is deployed to crack the hard shells of steamed crabs in order to expose and make the meat inside more accessible. Users should beware that excess force will crush the shells into tiny pieces, which will then get embedded in the delicate meat; an experienced crab eater will only tap the hammer at pressure points to break the shell, then use their hands or a fork (see lobster fork, page 156) to extract the meat in large pieces.

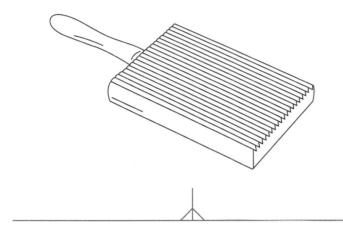

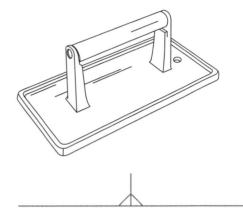

GNOCCHI BOARD

A special piece of equipment, the gnocchi board originated in Italy, where gnocchi—little pasta dumplings, often made of a mixture of flour and potato or ricotta cheese—were invented. The small rectangular board is usually made of wood and has a chunky handle. Most important, a gnocchi board has many parallel carved grooves on its surface, running from the handle to the opposite end of the board. This texture is the main purpose of the gnocchi board, as it gives the dumplings the shape and surface that they are known for. To use, one rolls the gnocchi dough into a rope and cuts the rope into small pieces. Then, holding the gnocchi board in the non-dominant hand, the cook presses each piece of dough against the board with the other hand so that the dough is marked by the grooves of the board on one side only. The other side of the gnocchi acquires a natural indentation in the shape of the maker's thumb. The texture that the gnocchi board provides, as well as the concavity of the pasta's overall shape, helps the sauce cling onto the cooked dumplings.

GRILL PRESS

A grill press is a heavy-duty weight, meant to press down on cooking food to help compress it and/or make it flush against its cooking surface. Often used for griddled sandwiches or bacon, a grill press is usually made of cast iron and has an offset handle made of metal or wood.

MEAT TENDERIZER

A meat tenderizer, also known as a meat mallet or meat pounder, is a tool used for tenderizing and flattening meats before cooking. There are multiple styles. The most common looks like a mallet, with a handle attached to a two-sided head; one side of the head is flat, and the other side has small blunted teeth. Using the flat side means only force will be used to tenderize, so it is best for more delicate meats like veal and chicken, while the jagged side uses its teeth to physically breakdown meat fibers, best for tough cuts of beef. Another style of tenderizer has a single face—which can be flat or textured—attached to a short handle on the back, like a stamp. This type of tenderizer gives more control to the user. Last but not least, a blade tenderizer uses a collection of tall thin blades held together by a mechanized handle and safeguard; one punches the blades down repeatedly to breakdown the muscular fibers of the meat.

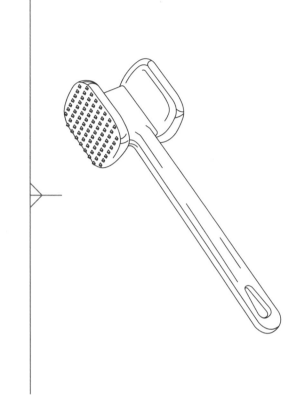

MOLCAJETE

The Mexican version of the mortar and pestle, a molcajete is a stone work bowl and pounding instrument, wonderful for hand-grinding foods. It dates back to the pre-Hispanic Mesoamerican cultures, including the Aztecs and the Mayans, and is traditionally made from vesicular basalt, a dark-colored volcanic rock that contains many small holes, though concrete or other stone is available as well. Molcajetes are intended for grinding spices but they can also be used for a wide variety of kitchen tasks including preparing salsas, moles, and guacamoles. The basalt version's porous nature means it can retain various flavors and transfer them between foods during the preparation process, an attribute sometimes credited in the distinct taste of the final dish.

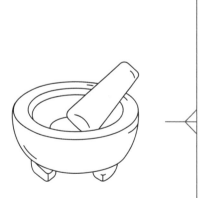

MORTAR & PESTLE

A mortar and pestle is an ancient two-part kitchen tool, meant to crush and grind ingredients using the blunt pounding instrument inside a sturdy thick-sided work bowl. Wonderful for grinding spices, crushing herbs, blending sauces, and more, the mortar and pestle gives cooks great control over the processing of foods, unlike a food processor—which is often called for in recipes as a good replacement and cuts rather than grinds. The two components are usually made of hard stone, ceramic, metal, or hardwood. The molcajete (opposite page) is the Mexican basalt version of a mortar and pestle.

Pesto's Origins

The Italian word *pesto*, a contracted version of the verb *pestare*, meaning to pound or crush, is related by definition and origin to the English word *pestle*. Italians often claim that making a pesto in anything other than a mortar and pestle will result in a different sauce, as the pounding of the basil and pinenuts releases the oils and crushes the ingredients, rather than mincing them, and the oil can be added slowly and gently incorporated, resulting in a silkier emulsification.

NUTCRACKER

A nutcracker opens nuts by cracking their hard outer shell to reveal the nut inside. The most common type of nutcracker functions like a pair of pliers: the shell is placed between the two concave sides of a metal clamp and is squeezed by hand to create enough pressure to split the shell. Another variation of nutcracker involves a screw mechanism, where the point of the screw is rotated and driven into the shell until it cracks.

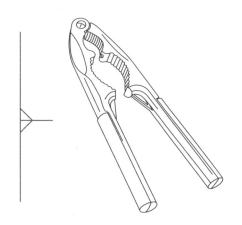

Decorative Nutcrackers

For centuries, a popular type of nutcracker has been the wooden solider or knight figurine, whose mouth opens to clamp down and crack open nuts. Not the most practical or functional, these types are not always strong enough to actually accomplish their purpose, so are mostly intended for decoration, especially around the Christmas holiday.

POTATO MASHER

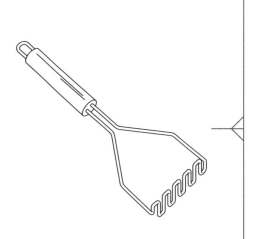

There are two different types of potato masher, a utensil used to crush cooked potatoes. The first is similar to a ricer, where a perforated metal disk attached to a handle is used to smash potatoes from above, forcing the food through the holes to create a mash. The handle is often perpendicular to the disk, though other designs have made the handle shorter and parallel to the disk, which allows for more direct pressure and control. The second type of masher swaps out the perforated disk for a plane of very heavy gauge wire in a zig zag design. To use, one presses the wire configuration upon the cooked potatoes to crush them, repeating until the mash reaches the desired consistency. The results of the first type are more like riced potatoes, while the second design gives a more rustic and inconsistent texture.

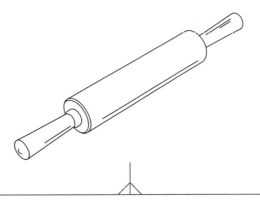

ROLLING PIN

A rolling pin is a long, cylindrical hand tool that one rolls and presses upon a ball of dough in order to flatten and shape it. There are two standard designs: one that you roll by placing your hands directly on the thick pin (also called a dowel), and one with handles that roll the dowel for you. Wooden pins are most common for home chefs, while professional chefs might also use a marble version—other materials exist, but are much less common. Both wooden and marble rolling pins have their benefits: a wooden version will hold dusting flour longer (depending on the type of wood, which determines porousness), making it good for rolling out sticky doughs. A marble version will stay cold, making it ideal for working with pastry that needs to be kept cool. Some newer rolling pins include removable, multi-size bands or rings that wrap around the edges of the pin, which offer an easy way to roll the dough to a desired thickness.

A Variety of Pins

There are a variety of rolling pins, and cooks have different allegiances and notions as to which is the best type. Straight and French pins are related, certainly, as the only difference between them is the tapering of the ends of the simple dowel. Roller-style pins are most common in American kitchens. Embossed, striated, or otherwise decorated pins are best for specialized baking, where one might press the pin across already rolled-out dough to imprint a pattern or texture onto it prior to cooking.

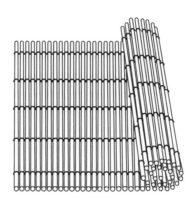

SUSHI MAT

Constructed out of a set of parallel bamboo skewers bound together neatly with string, a sushi mat is a square-shaped flexible mat that measures around 8 inches in length and 8 inches in width, give or take a few inches. Both professional sushi chefs and at-home cooks use a sushi mat to form Maki: Japanese seaweed rolls. To use, one lays a piece of nori (dried seaweed) onto the mat and tops with a short, thin layer of seasoned sushi rice; chosen toppings (raw fish; cooked fish; slices of omelet; or raw, cooked, or pickled vegetables) are placed on top of the rice in a horizontal line. One then picks up the edge of the mat to help pull the edge of the seaweed tightly

over the rest of the ingredients, and then continues to roll until the seaweed has folded back onto itself (moistening the edge with a bit of water helps to hold the finished roll closed), forming a sealed seaweed roll with open sides. The mat is especially helpful as the nori is toasted prior to rolling, and has a crispy, delicate texture that would be hard to manipulate with one's fingers alone. Sometimes the cook will cover the mat in plastic wrap to prevent any ingredients from sticking to it, but it is not necessary. The finished Maki are usually cut into slices so the diner can see a crosscut of the beautifully arranged ingredients inside.

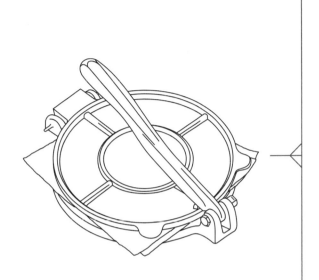

TORTILLA PRESS

A tortilla press is a mechanical device made to form corn tortillas, alleviating the need to form them by hand or by using a rolling pin. Often constructed of two heavy cast-iron plates connected by a hinge, the tortilla press flattens a ball of dough into a thin pancake (usually about an $\frac{1}{8}$ of an inch thick, or thinner) by using a hand-operated lever to press the cast-iron plates together, flattening whatever is held between them. The dough is a simple mixture of masa harina (ground nixtamalized cornmeal), salt, and water. To keep the dough from sticking to the iron plates, sheets of plastic wrap or parchment paper are sandwiched around the dough ball before it is put between the plates. Traditionally, the finished tortillas are cooked on a comal (page 77), though a griddle or another pan could easily be substituted.

Forming Flour Tortillas

While a tortilla press is the ideal device for making corn tortillas easily and quickly, the same cannot be said for flour tortillas. The dough of a flour tortilla is made from a blend of flour and fat that should not be worked too thoroughly in order to ensure the dough stays pliable and doesn't turn tough. Squashing this more delicate dough in a press is not ideal. Hand rolling using a trusty rolling pin is usually the method and tool of choice for creating the perfectly textured flour tortilla.

Gadgets

Gadgets are used in the kitchen to break down or process food in particular ways. While some foods are ready to eat as is, others need a little prep before consuming, whether that involves removing the skin, seeds, or pits, or reshaping the product. Some have sharp edges or blades, meant to open, slice, peel, or shred. Others are designed to grind, mash, or beat food into submission. There are even some gadgets used to apply heat or smoke to food.

APPLE CORER

An apple corer is a manual tool used to remove the seed pocket of an apple. The corer consists of a short tube with a sharp, serrated end, attached to a handle. To use, the corer is plunged down through the center of the apple, cutting a cylinder of seeds from the surrounding flesh; the corer is then removed, pulling the seed cylinder with it, which can then be discarded. An apple cutter is a similar tool which functions like an apple corer, but also includes additional blades to cut the apple flesh into sections with the same downward stroke. Pears and quinces can also be cored with an apple corer.

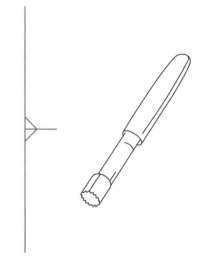

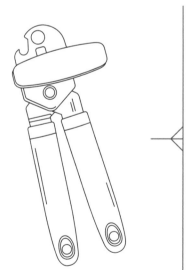

CAN OPENER

Multiple varieties of a can opener have been in existence since cans were invented in the eighteenth century, but two remain popular: the rotating-wheel style that removes the entire lid of the can, and a church key, which cuts a small opening in the lid, suitable only for liquids. The rotating wheel version operates by clamping two wheels (one sharp one for cutting, one serrated one for gripping) around the can's rim, and twisting a key to spin the wheels and move the opener around the perimeter, the sharp wheel cutting around the interior edge as it goes. The church key opener functions like a lever: it hooks to the edge of the can then, by tipping the handle upward, the pointed tip of the opener is forced downward into the can, cutting a triangular hole.

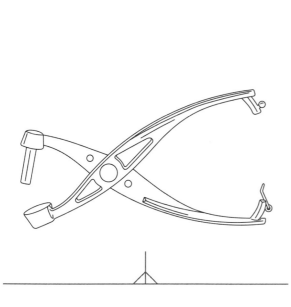

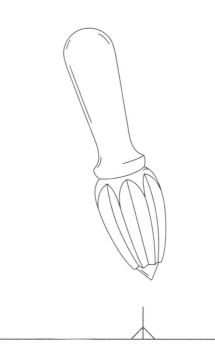

CHERRY & OLIVE PITTER

Cherry and olive pitters, also called cherry and olive stoners, are not always marketed as a single tool, but functionally and visually they are the same: meant to remove the pit from the inside of the fruit while keeping the physical integrity of the fruit mostly intact. Similar to a garlic press, the tool is a hinged utensil with a bowl on one arm to hold the olive or cherry and a thin blunted rod on the other; the bowl has a hole in the bottom. To use, the fruit is added to the bowl and the arms are closed together, forcing the rod through the fruit and the bowl's hole, pushing the pit out in one motion; the pit ejects through the hole. Most pitters are spring loaded so that the punch is more rapid.

CITRUS REAMER

Like a citrus squeezer (page 208), the citrus reamer is a tool for extracting juice from citrus fruits. The reamer is a conical bulb with wide grooves, which tapers to a slightly blunted point at one end and is attached to a chunky handle or base on the other. When the halved fruit is twisted upon the reamer, the convex edges puncture and scrape the fruit flesh, and the channels between those edges provide a passage for the juice to drip into your chosen container. The reamer comes in both a tabletop version (manual or electric), which is normally made of plastic or metal, where the fruit is pressed upon it and twisted around the reamer, or a handheld version, usually wood or metal, where one hand holds the reamer and the other the fruit to be juiced. Because the diameter of the handheld reamer is small, it works best with smaller citrus like lemons and limes.

CITRUS SQUEEZER

The citrus squeezer is a two-armed, hinged gadget with matching molded hemispherical bowls shaped to clamp around a halved citrus fruit—usually lemons or limes—thereby extracting the juice from the fruit by force. The bottom bowl of the squeezer has perforations that allow only the juice to drip through; when finished, the squeezer is opened and the seeds and spent rind are removed for disposal.

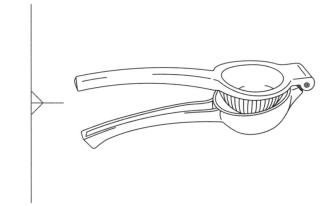

Citrus Boost

To yield the most juice from your citrus in a citrus squeezer, put the fruit in cut side down. It seems counterintuitive, as the nested bowls of the squeezer are concave and seem designed to hug the fruit, but flipping the half upside down will give more copious results.

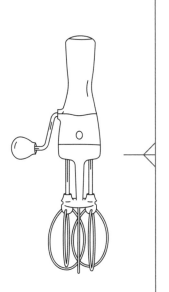

EGGBEATER

An eggbeater is a manual gadget that is used to beat eggs and egg whites. Consisting of two rotary beaters connected to a hand crank, the eggbeater works by holding the handle of the egg beater upright and stable, while turning the crank with the other hand; the beaters, which are pointed into a bowl or vessel of ingredients, then turn on their axel and agitate the food. The faster the crank turns, the faster the beaters turn. In addition to eggs (for omelets), or egg whites (for meringues or angel food cakes), eggbeaters are an excellent device to use for making whipped cream. The eggbeater has fallen somewhat out of fashion as electric beaters and/or stand mixers have gained popularity with home cooks. Though these electronic appliances are able to quickly accomplish the same tasks, the eggbeater is still an excellent choice as one doesn't need to drag a bulky appliance out from the depths of your kitchen cabinets. As an added bonus (of sorts), the egg beater offers the benefit of working out one's arm muscles.

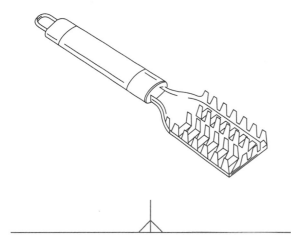

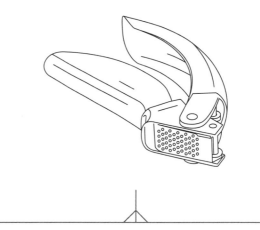

FISH SCALER/UROKOTORI

A fish scaler's purpose is to remove the inedible scales from a raw whole fish without damaging its skin. It is constructed from a piece of metal with jagged teeth, connected to a handle, and comes in a variety of styles and shapes. One uses the scaler by repeatedly pulling it across the skin of the fish from tail to head. Since most fish are descaled prior to sale on the retail market, this tool is used primarily by anglers, commercial outlets, and restaurant kitchens rather than in regular home use. A *urokotori* is a Japanese fish scaler, sometimes made of brass.

GARLIC PRESS

Similar to a citrus squeezer (opposite page), a garlic press is a two-handled, hinged gadget meant to mash individual cloves of garlic. A small, perforated cavity is located on one arm near the hinge, and the other arm has a movable press that fits snugly into the cavity. To use, the press is opened up, a garlic clove is inserted into the cavity, and the two arms are brought together, with the press pushing the garlic in the cavity, forcing it through the holes. Peeling the garlic clove before adding it to the press yields more crushed garlic than unpeeled, but either way will work.

KITCHEN BLOW TORCH

A miniature version of its metalworking counterpart, a kitchen blow torch, also known as a culinary or cooking blow torch, is a butane-burning handheld tool that creates a powerful, localized flame and allows its operator to toast, melt, caramelize, flame roast, and sear foods. The flame is adjustable and switches on and off by way of a finger operated trigger. Best used for small, specific jobs, a kitchen blow torch is especially adept at toasting meringue on top of a pie or caramelizing sugar on top of a custard to make crème brûlée. A kitchen blow torch can also be wielded to crisp up chicken skin or roasted vegetables, making it a popular addition to a food stylist's arsenal.

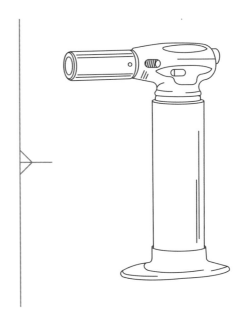

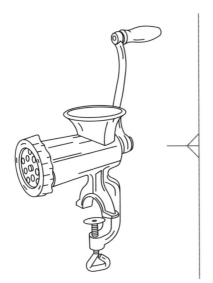

MEAT GRINDER

A meat grinder is a device that mills meat and other foods into mince. There are mechanical, hand-cranked versions as well as electric versions, including a popular attachment for stand mixers. A meat grinder works by loading the attached funnel with pieces of meat, then cranking the handle to force the meat through the machine, first though the internal screw conveyor, then out through a perforated plate. The number and size of perforations of the plate determine the fineness of the mince. One can also add seasonings and flavorings to the machine with the meat. There are attachments that let the user push the finished ground meat directly into casings for sausage.

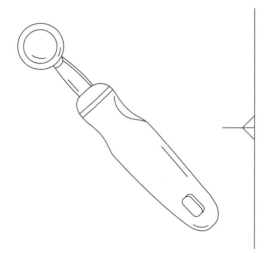

MELON BALLER

Like a miniature ice cream scoop, a melon baller is a semicircular utensil used to measure out ball-shaped bites of melon from the whole fruit. Melon ballers require scooping the fruit in a particular way; twisting the head of the baller to create a full sphere. Some models include a spring-loaded handle to make ejecting the melon from the baller easier; others are two headed, with a small and large side. The melon baller works with all types of melon—watermelon, cantaloupe, honeydew, etc.—as well as some other soft and yielding foods, like butter or ice cream.

MILK FROTHER

Given the popularity of cappuccinos, lattes, and other specialty coffeehouse drinks, it's no surprise that in the last few years, milk frothers have found a place in the at-home coffee-making supplies market. These small electric machines are able to quickly whip up milk foam for topping various drinks, and some are able to heat or chill a beverage as well. The simplest and most common format is a handheld, battery powered version that includes a handle with a small interior motor and button controls. This handle is attached to a vertical wand that ends in a tiny, circle-shaped whisk covered in a tight coil of wire. When turned on, the spinning of the whisk aerates the liquid in which it is submerged, creating bubbles; after a few seconds, the bubbles build up to create dollops of foam. (Be sure you submerge the frother before turning it on, otherwise you may end up with a milk covered kitchen.) In addition to creating froth, these small machines are also adept at thoroughly blending powders (like cocoa powder, protein powder, etc.) into fluids, whipping eggs, and emulsifying liquid ingredients. Other milk frother formats include manual versions that look like a French press, which pumps air into milk by hand, and electric versions that hold the milk as well as the mechanics, automatically delivering a finished product ready to top a beverage.

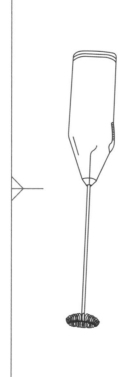

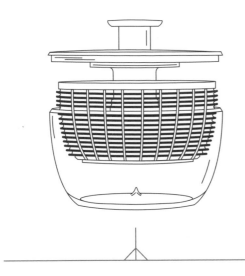

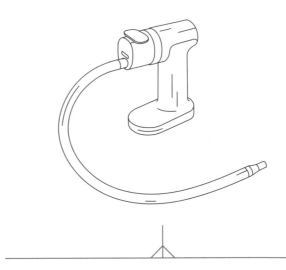

SALAD SPINNER

A salad spinner is a very helpful tool to aid in washing and drying lettuce or other leafy greens. It is made of three components: an outer bowl (often plastic or thin metal), a removable colander, and a lid that contains a mechanism to make the colander spin when assembled. The mechanism is either a pull-string or a pump; the pump version also has a brake button to quickly stop the spinning. To use, one fills the bowl and colander with cold water and lettuce, agitates the lettuce in the water to wash it, then lifts the colander out to drain the lettuce. To fully dry the lettuce, place the colander of washed lettuce back in the empty bowl and top with the lid, then spin the colander a couple of times. Centrifugal force radiates the water away from the greens, sending it toward the sides of the bowl, where it drips down to the bottom for easy disposal. After a couple spins, pour out any water that has accumulated in the bottom of the bowl.

SMOKE INFUSER/SMOKING GUN

A smoke infuser, also known as a smoking gun, is a small handheld battery-operated appliance that generates smoke in order to imbue food or drinks with its essence. As opposed to smoking with an outdoor smoker—a large contained vessel, similar to a grill, whose use requires time and a lot of fuel—a smoke infuser is an indoor option which can be turned on and wielded immediately without any fuss. To use, fill the infuser's chamber with just a few wood chips, dried flowers, tea, or other burnable substances, and light it. Then point the attached nozzle or tube, from which smoke should be streaming, into a bowl or other container with the food to be smoked: meats, cheeses, drinks, and more. For best results, tightly cover the vessel to contain the smoke and create a sealed atmosphere; the denser the smoke, and the longer food is exposed to it, the smokier the flavor will be. One major difference between this appliance and its larger outdoor relative is that the smoke infuser applies smoke to food for flavor only; the heat of the smoke and short duration of its contact with the food means that food needs to be fully cooked separately.

Salad Spinning Alternatives

While a salad spinner is a tool that both washes and dries lettuce and other greens, there are other ways to clean one's salad fodder without this particularly bulky piece of equipment. A large mixing bowl (page 100) or a sparkling clean sink with a stopper can provide enough space to hold a significant amount of greens and a sufficient volume of cold water required to properly clean the leaves and loosen any grit. (Do not be tempted to spray down the greens in a colander [page 217], which does a poor job; submerging them in water is the only way to thoroughly clean them.) Allowing the leaves to soak in the water for a few minutes and gently swishing them is helpful in loosening dirt. If the greens are especially dirty or sandy, changing the water once or twice may be necessary. Once clean, lifting the clean greens from the bowl or sink is best as pouring the greens directly into a colander to drain means potentially re-dirtying them with the grit that collects at the bottom of the bowl. When removing from the sink, always give the salad greens a preliminary shake to remove any excess water. From this point, there are a couple of options for drying the greens. One option is to place them in a single layer on clean kitchen towels (page 115) or paper towels and then to roll them up. The surface area of the cloth will absorb most of the water, thereby drying the greens. These rolls can then be placed directly in the crisper drawer in your refrigerator (page 35) and stored thusly for a couple of days. Another option is to place the damp greens in a clean cotton pillowcase (or carefully rolled and wrapped large kitchen towel), securely grab the open end to close, then swing the pillowcase around like a lasso. The centrifugal force of spinning the greens will repel the water, wicking it away from the greens and onto the cloth surrounding it. Clean and dry greens, with flair to spare!

Graters, Mills & Sieves

Graters, the rough or perforated surfaces on which one rubs a variety of foods to be broken down into shreds, gratings, or slices, have many forms. A grater's size, shape, and number of sharpened holes determine what ingredients it is best suited to, ranging from cheese, vegetables, chocolate, fruits, spices, and more. Some graters can stand on their own while others must be held in your hand. Sieves and mills are kitchen gear that share a porous form—a weave of strong material, like metal, or a perforated piece of plastic, metal, or wood—which use gravity or manual force to strain, drain, sift, or grind food.

BOX GRATER

A box grater is a standing tool with a handle on top and multiple flat sides that feature a selection of variously shaped sharp holes and slots that may be used for grating and slicing. To manipulate this tool, one holds the grater still by gripping the top handle then brushing an ingredient against one of the sides of the grater using firm strokes. This will allow you to shave off the surface of the ingredient, sending the shavings tumbling inside the cavity of the grater for collection. Most commonly there are four sides to a box grater (hence the name), but graters can have anywhere from three to eight sides. Most graters include large holes ideal for creating large long shreds; small holes for making fine long shreds; wide slits, sometimes with a decorative wavy edge, for making thin slices; and small starburst-shaped outward-facing perforations for producing the finest gratings. In addition to grating things into shards, slices, and powder, the box grater is also able to break down softer ingredients entirely; for example, tomato halves, when grated on the large holes of a box grater, become pulp.

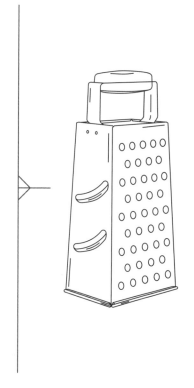

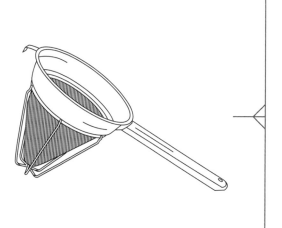

CHINOIS

A chinois is a classic French kitchen tool, a large conical-shaped sieve of very fine mesh, strong enough to withstand the pressure of forcing foods through it. A specially shaped conical pestle is sometimes sold with the chinois to aid in pushing foods through the mesh. The chinois is best used for creating purees or as a means to strain away fine particles from a sauce, soup, or stock. In a pinch, it can also be used to sift dry ingredients, but the fineness of its weave means that only the smallest particles will be able to pass through the mesh.

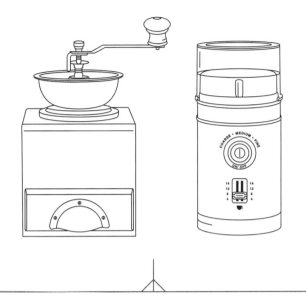

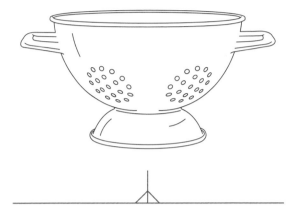

COFFEE GRINDER

A coffee grinder is a small motorized machine meant to grind roasted coffee beans into powders of various levels of coarseness. Consisting of a small rotating blade nestled inside of an electric-powered canister, a coffee grinder can be used to grind coffee beans as well as other hard foodstuffs, like rice and spices, though you may notice some cross contamination of flavors if you opt to use your coffee grinder for other purposes. Manual coffee grinders, once considered old-fashioned, are experiencing an uptick in popularity with today's DIY coffee culture. Similar to a pepper grinder (page 221), these handheld devices grind using a set of burrs that are turned via a crank handle.

COLANDER

The colander is a multipurpose strainer that is usually made of perforated metal though recent versions have been made using silicone and plastic. While the gauge and number of holes varies, the main purpose for all colanders is the same: to wash and strain foods. Whether the job is to strain the juice from a can of tomatoes or to drain a pot of cooked pasta, the colander is meant to allow liquids to pass through its holes. If you want a finer strain, use a sieve (page 223). A colander is also a common tool for washing produce or rinsing larger ingredients. In a pinch, a small colander can also be placed into a large lidded pot to double as a steamer. Since most colanders are made from light metal such as aluminum or stainless steel, they are heatproof and very durable.

The Colander As a Cooking Tool

In addition to draining and washing, the colander has another off-label use: making German spaetzle, a freeform egg-noodle dumpling. Specific spaetzle makers exist, but if single-use kitchen tools aren't welcome in your house, a large-holed colander makes a fine substitute. The batter is viscous enough to be able to be placed in the bowl of a colander set over simmering water and pressed through using a rubber or silicone scraper: the thick drops will scatter into the water and cook.

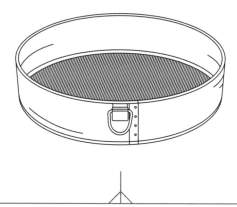

DRUM SIEVE

As its name implies, the drum sieve is a flat strainer used primarily in professional kitchens, where the mesh is stretched across a round frame, like a snare drum; it is also known as a *tamis* (pronounced "tammy"). Its shape is meant for resting easily over the rim of a bowl, where one can easily refine ingredients or mixtures by scraping horizontally with a pestle (page 199), spoon, or bowl scraper to force the food through its weave. Its wide surface area makes quick work of most jobs. It comes in a variety of gauges, able to make fine to coarse purees and to remove skins, seeds, and other bits of impurities from a sauce, coulis, or paste. The drum sieve is also used as a sifter, where the edge of the drum sieve can be easily tapped against one's hand to release dry milled ingredients, such as flours and sugars, through its mesh.

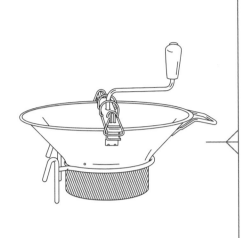

FOOD MILL

Dating back to the 1930s, the food mill—also known as a passatutto, purée sieve, moulinette, mouli légumes, or passe-vite—is a simple and effective manual tool used to mash and sieve soft foods in order to remove seeds or pulp to produce a smooth puree. Depending on the ingredient, the food mill can function like a blender, food processer, or a sieve. Hung over the lip of a bowl, the food mill operates with a crank, which rotates a blade over a perforated disk in the bottom of the mill, pushing the food through. Most versions of the food mill come with interchangeable discs perforated by holes of varying size, number, and shape, allowing greater control over the degree to which the food is refined. The food mill is usually made of stainless steel or aluminum, but can sometimes be made of plastic, especially for smaller versions advertised for making baby food.

MICROPLANE/RASP GRATER

Generally known as a rasp grater, the Microplane is also the brand name of these very sharp handheld graters. With a long, thin grating surface perforated with very small slits or holes, a Microplane is best used for fine jobs that require the increased agility that a handheld grater provides. As such, a Microplane is often used tableside. Microplanes are best at zesting citrus fruits, grating hard cheeses into fine light shreds, and grating chocolate.

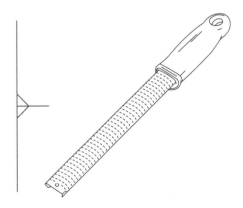

Kitchen vs. Studio

The design of a Microplane is based on a rasp, a tool used in woodworking and ceramics. In those fields, a rasp is used as an active tool—rubbing its perforated surface onto wood or clay to shape it via reduction; the shards created in this process are debris destined for the waste bin. Interestingly, cooks use a Microplane in the opposite way, manipulating ingredients upon it and collecting the shards for use.

NUTMEG GRATER

A nutmeg grater is a very small, perforated grater, sometimes in a semi-cylindrical form, usually with a small handle. It is used primarily for grating hard spices like nutmeg, but in a pinch can be used for other small jobs, like zesting fruit. A Microplane or the finest side of a box grater can be used instead of a nutmeg grater if one is unavailable.

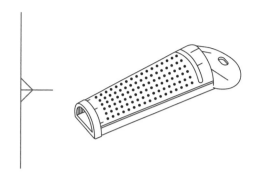

BYONG

In the eighteenth century, it was fashionable for men to carry nutmeg in a pocket-sized silver container equipped with a grater in order to add freshly grated nutmeg to punch. These days, nutmeg graters are still sometimes used by bartenders to garnish drinks with the freshly grated spice.

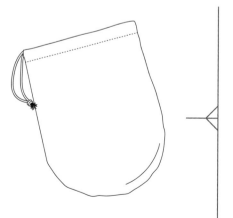

NUT MILK BAG

A nut milk bag is a fine-mesh filter in the form of a bag, used to drain ground beans, nuts, or grains when acquiring their "milk," such as in the case of making soy milk or almond milk. To use, one combines the chosen ingredient with water in a blender (page 38) or similar device, and then grind the ingredients until very fine. After the mixture steeps, the amalgam is added to a nut milk bag and suspended in or above a vessel. The bag filters out the silty fine particles, leaving the finished, pulp- and silt-free milk ready to drink.

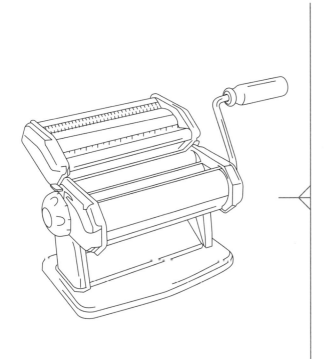

PASTA MACHINE

A pasta machine is a device made to roll fresh pasta dough into thin sheets. The manual version consists of two rollers operated by a crank; the distance between the rollers, which can be adjusted, determines the thickness of the pasta sheets. When starting with a ball of dough, one starts the machine on the widest setting and runs the dough through, folding between passes, until a thick consistent sheet is made. Then one progressively adjusts the roller's levels to make the sheets thinner and thinner. These sheets can be used as is to make lasagna, or cut down with a knife or stamped into other shapes. Some versions of the pasta machine have additional specialized rollers to cut the sheets into noodles or to press into small ravioli. Pasta machines can also be electric; a popular electric version is an attachment to the stand mixer.

PEPPER MILL

A pepper mill, also called a pepper grinder, is a handheld burr mill meant to grind whole peppercorns directly into a pan or onto a plate. Usually operated by turning the top with one hand while holding the bottom stationary, a pepper mill functions by crushing whole peppercorns between its two interior abrasive surfaces. Most versions of a pepper mill can be adjusted to create a range from cracked to finely ground pepper. Electric versions often include a container for the ground pepper, so one can grind and measure larger quantities.

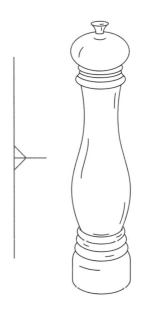

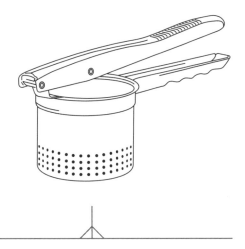

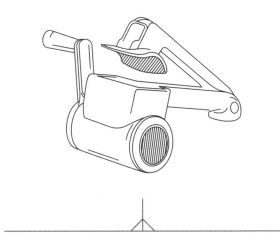

RICER

Like a larger garlic press (page 209), a ricer forces pieces of soft food through a perforated cavity in order to mash them. One of the two hinged arms contains a perforated cavity, the other a press that fits inside the cavity. By squeezing the two hinged arms together, the press, placed upon the food in the cavity, pushes the food through the perforations, extruding mashed food out of the bottom. The name stems from the fact that the holes' size creates a mash that has the consistency and size of rice. A food mill (page 219) also creates "riced" food, and thus the two gadgets' names are often interchanged, though some argue that a ricer is best used on potatoes, while a food mill can be used on a wider variety of vegetables.

ROTARY GRATER

A specialized mechanical grater, also called a cheese grater, the rotary grater is a simple handheld tool used for grating medium-hard to hard cheese. Featuring a perforated drum and an adjustable arm to hold and press the cheese against it, the rotary grater is held in one hand while the other turns a crank that spins the drum; because the cheese is pressed against the drum, this motion creates cheese gratings or shards that collect inside the drum. The size and shape of the gratings depends on the size and shape of the perforations. While specifically created for cheese, chocolate can work in these graters as well.

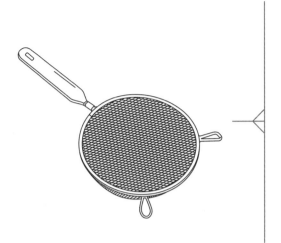

SIEVE

A sieve is a mesh strainer, most often used to pass ingredients through its weave to sift or puree them. The mesh weave can range from fine to coarse; fine sieves sift flour and other dry ingredients, coarse sieves can be used as a basket to wash produce. Fine and coarse sieves can also strain ingredients to make purees and pastes of varying smoothness by forcing the food through its mesh using a bowl-shaped scraper or pestle. Sieves are also used to separate solids from liquids; for example, one would use a small sieve to strain the pulp from freshly squeezed juice.

SIFTER

Often used in baking, a sifter is a fine mesh strainer used to refine and break up clumps of various ingredients such as powdered sugar, flour, or cocoa powder. A sifter works by aerating ingredients, thus allowing them to be fully incorporated into a larger mixture or batter. There are a variety of formats. A simple sifter can be just a bowl-shaped sieve with a handle; you can tap the edge of the sifter to agitate ingredients through the mesh. Another basic model is the sifter shaker, which efficiently filters ingredients when you turn the shaker upside down and shake. More complex versions, often canister-shaped with a vertical handle, employ additional features such as a squeezable mechanism that agitates the ingredients or a crank that spins, pushing the ingredient through the mesh. It is important to keep the sifter out of the way of moisture when using, as liquid will counteract the functionality by causing the ingredients to stick and further clump.

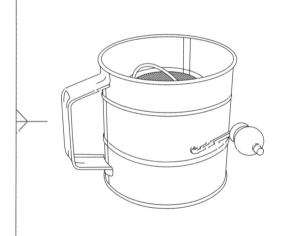

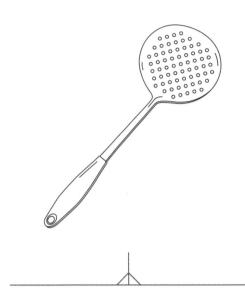

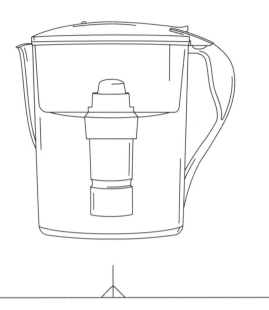

SPOON SIEVE

The spoon sieve is a wide and shallow mesh or perforated spoon with a long handle. The mesh version is the best tool for skimming, like when removing the scum off the surface of a simmering stock, or for sifting small amounts of ingredients, such as powdered sugar over a cake. The perforated version, sometimes called a French spoon sieve, is best for removing ingredients from a hot liquid, similar in function to a spider (page 244) or slotted spoon (page 242). Perforated spoon sieves can be made of silver, brass, copper, wood, aluminum, or other metals, and are sometimes covered in colored enamel; mesh spoon sieves are made of metal and come in a variety of gauges.

WATER FILTER

A water filter—specifically a home-use system—is a device intended to remove impurities and lingering off-tastes from tap water. Usually comprised of a pitcher with a built-in filtration system, a water filter works simply: the drinker adds water directly to a holding compartment stationed above the base of the pitcher then, as water is poured in, gravity pulls it through the filter, dripping now-purified water into the pitcher below. Once the water has been filtered, the pitcher is ready to dispense clean water in a glass for drinking and may be kept on the counter or in the refrigerator (page 35), depending on the water temperature desired. Styles vary, as do the intricacies of the systems themselves. Most water filters are made from plastic or glass, and the filter itself is often replaceable. This type of residential water filter is not to be mistaken for a full water filtration system, which is used for making contaminated water potable, either on a municipal scale or for individual use when camping or hiking.

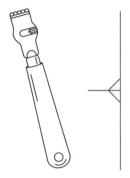

ZESTER

A zester is a small handheld tool used to remove very thin delicate strips of zest from citrus fruit. The tip of the metal head includes sharp small holes, which one strokes over the surface of the fruit, applying pressure, to create the pieces of zest. A zester often includes a channel knife on the same tool, which cuts a deeper, thicker piece of zest; bartenders use these strips to garnish drinks.

An Array of Zest

Citrus zest is a wonderful way to get the concentrated flavor of citrus oils into drinks, baked goods, and sweet and savory cooking. Depending on its end use, the size and texture of the zest should be considered, and the three main tools for acquiring zest—a zester, a channel knife, and a Microplane—provide different options. A channel knife cuts a thick, grooved piece of zest that includes a bit of the pith, which can be curled and used for a drink's non-edible garnish. A zester creates individualized strips of zest, thinner than that from a channel knife, with no pith, and can vary in length. These strips work well in baked goods (like in cakes or cookies, where one can see the zest) or as an edible garnish. A Microplane (page 219) creates the finest citrus zest—which comes out almost fluffy—good to use in cooking and baking where the cook wants the flavor of citrus without a noticeable or visible texture.

Knives & Sharpeners

CHEESE KNIFE

CHEF'S KNIFE

CLEAVER

FILLET KNIFE

GRAPEFRUIT KNIFE

HONING STEEL

KNIFE BLOCK

KNIFE SHARPENER

KNIFE STRIP

MEZZALUNA

PARING KNIFE

SERRATED KNIFE

TOMATO KNIFE

WHETSTONE

It could be argued that sharp edges are the most important tools in a kitchen, as they are able to breakdown a raw product (vegetables, meat, fish, etc.) into useable pieces, ready to be eaten directly or cooked. While a chef's knife or cleaver is used by almost all cooks, and is multipurpose enough to do at least an adequate job on most tasks, other sharp items, like a grapefruit knife or a cheese cutter, are quite specialized and useful for only certain situations or ingredients.

CHEESE KNIFE

A cheese knife is a knife that is specifically used for cutting cheese. The large professional type often differentiates itself from other knives by various design features—etched blades or blades with die-cut holes or slots—to prevent the cheese from sticking to the knife's blade; their edges range from rounded to serrated. They can be single handled, or large and double handled, for commercial use. There are also small household cheese knives used for serving on a communal cheese plate. Usually sold in sets of three or more, these cheese knives are shaped with a specific type of cheese in mind: spreaders for soft cheeses, a spade for firm cheeses, and a plane for firm or semi soft cheeses, among others.

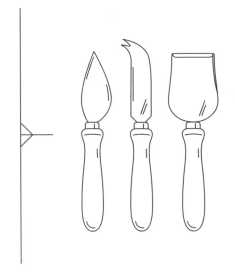

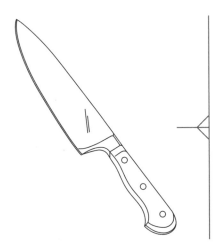

CHEF'S KNIFE

A chef's knife is the most multipurpose knife in a western kitchen, and despite its name, it is the most common knife for home cooks as well as professionals. Its heavy blade with a pointed tip is able to do most prep tasks, from slicing, dicing, and chopping, to cutting apart large cuts of meat and splitting hard produce like pumpkins. The length of the blade varies from 6 to 12 inches, and users should pick a size that feels comfortable in their hand. Though one size should be sufficient, some cooks like to have a smaller size for more intricate jobs and a larger size for bigger tasks.

Necessary Knives

There is a seemingly endless supply of knife designs, but if you are short on space or money, or prefer a streamlined kitchen, focus on the three most important and multipurpose knives to get through food preparation: a chef's knife or cleaver, a paring knife, and a serrated knife. Between these three, you can chop, mince, carve, slice, peel, section, and even breakdown large cuts of meat and produce.

Cleaver Hacks

One might think of a cleaver for only big jobs in the kitchen, like chopping bones, but it also excels at everyday kitchen tasks, like mincing, as well as a few unusual actions not normally advertised. For example, the blunt edge of the head can be used to pound and tenderize meat, since a cleaver is so heavy. The wide flat surface of the blade can be used to scoop and transfer cut ingredients from your cutting board to another vessel. And that same flat surface can also be used to crush small ingredients like garlic and ginger.

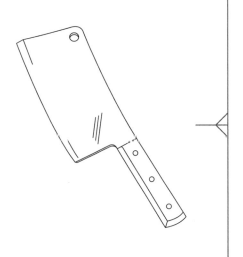

CLEAVER

A cleaver, similar to a hatchet, is a large, heavy knife: a flat rectangular blade with one sharpened edge, attached to a long handle. Its design makes it the best sharp edge for cutting apart large cuts of meat, as one can swing it down on the food and hack it apart. The head of the cleaver is hefty and strong, to add weight to each swing, making it able to cut through bone as well as thick cartilage and dense meat—hence its common association with butchers. That said, lighter versions (sometimes called Chinese cleavers or Chinese chef's knives) can also be used for regular chopping, slicing, mincing, and most other kitchen tasks, making it a multipurpose tool.

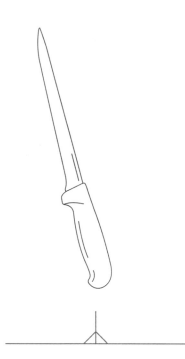

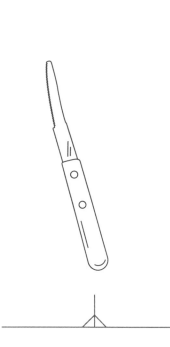

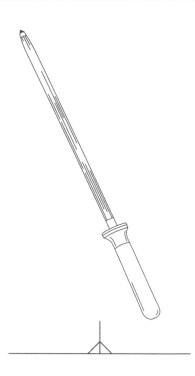

FILLET KNIFE

A fillet knife is used primarily for removing the skin and bones from a whole fish. It has a very long, skinny blade, flexible enough to bend, that slides easily between the skin and body of the fish without marring the delicate flesh. Its sharp tip can be used to remove bones.

GRAPEFRUIT KNIFE

A grapefruit knife is a small specialty knife with a serrated blade designed specifically to separate the sections of a grapefruit from its tough membranes and skin. The shape of the blade is slightly curved, so as to be able to cut under as well as around each section of the fruit.

HONING STEEL

A honing steel is a steel rod with a handle that is used to hone kitchen knives, and is often included in knife sets; it is sometimes referred to as a sharpening steel or honing rod. Many erroneously classify the tool as a sharpener, but a honing rod is not able to sharpen knives so much as hone, or realign, them. As knives are used, the sharp edge begins to collapse or curl to one side; a honing rod resets the blade, straightening it, which gives the impression of renewed sharpness.

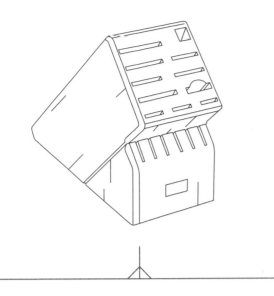

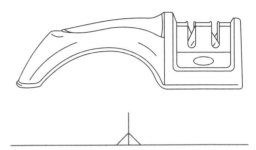

KNIFE BLOCK

Much safer than keeping one's prep knives in a drawer—where a hand can easily brush against a blade—a knife block is a holder for sharp knives that sits on the countertop. The knife block, a three-dimensional hunk or composite of wood, features multiple slots on its face that will fit a variety of different-size knives. Most standard knife blocks include large slots for a chef's knife (page 228) and a serrated knife (page 234), as well as a smaller slot for a paring knife (page 233), a thicker slot for kitchen shears (page 266), and a smaller hole for a honing steel (opposite page). When a knife is inserted into its chosen slot, the blade of the knife is completely hidden in the knife block, and the only part left exposed is the handle. Sometimes a knife block will be merchandised with a set of knives, specially designed so that each slot has a coordinating knife. Another more contemporary style of knife block presents a more universal solution: a container filled with tightly packed plastic rods, each about the circumference of a thick piece of spaghetti. When inserted, the knife's blade can easily slip between and among the rods, which hold the knife in place. This newfangled design can hold a much wider array of knife sizes and styles.

KNIFE SHARPENER

A knife sharpener comes in both a manual and an electric version, is designed to re-sharpen knives that have dulled with use. Though there are a variety of different sharpener designs, most share the same components: a coarse slot and a fine slot. The coarse slot works by dragging the knife blade a few times through the slot, applying some pressure, while stones on either side of the slot are actually grinding a very small amount of steel off the knife to create a new sharp edge. The fine side works similarly, but you do not apply pressure as you drag the knife through; this slot hones and realigns the already sharp blade. This two-step process should always be done in order from coarse to fine.

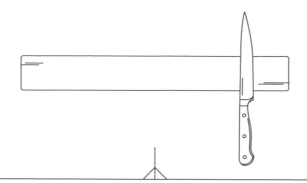

KNIFE STRIP

Similar in purpose to a knife block, a knife strip is a long, skinny magnetic panel that is mounted on a wall and serves as a place to store sharp knives. Stowing any metal bladed knife then becomes as easy as sticking a blade onto the magnetized strip, which will then hold the knife in place. The benefits of a knife strip are manifold: since the knives are entirely exposed, one can easily see and therefore quickly choose the correct knife for completing any given kitchen task. This is a much more difficult undertaking when using a knife block, as the only visible part of the knives are the handles. Knife strips are also less apt to dull or damage their cargo, especially when compared to storing knives in a drawer. Also, using a knife strip frees up valuable counter space. Finally, in addition to knives, the magnetic knife strip can also hold other metal utensils and gadgets, like whisks (pages 272–273), spatulas (pages 251 and 254), even measuring cups.

Sharpening, Two Ways

There are two common options when it comes to sharpening a kitchen knife: a whetstone (page 235) and a knife sharpener (above). A knife sharpener is a device (sometimes mechanical and sometimes electric) that is designed to do most of the work for you, and to do it fast. A whetstone is a simpler and older kitchen tool that requires a hands-on technique and a few additional minutes, but provides more exacting results. The control that a whetstone offers is likely the reason why most chefs and professional cooks will use a whetstone to sharpen what is arguably their most important tool—the knife—rather than an electric or manual sharpener. Note also that a whetstone can sharpen shears (page 266) and cleavers (page 229), as well as a knife of any type, blade size, or style (Eastern or Western), while a knife sharpener can sharpen only Western knives.

MEZZALUNA

A mezzaluna is a knife with a curved, half-moon-shaped blade; each end of the blade has a handle, so to use it, both hands are needed to rock the blade side to side over the food. The most common models have a single blade, but it can also be made with two or three blades; occasionally it comes with a special indented cutting board. The mezzaluna is best for quickly chopping or mincing ingredients such as herbs or garlic. The word *mezzaluna*, translated from Italian, means "half-moon," which reflects the shape of this utensil's blade.

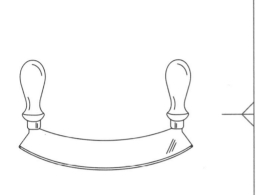

PARING KNIFE

Small but mighty, the paring knife is a short stout knife with a sharp blade and stubby handle. The tip of the knife can be either rounded or pointed. The paring knife is an essential tool for smaller and more detailed jobs in the kitchen: peeling and cutting vegetables and fruits, scoring, turning, and other precision cuts. It should feel like an extension of the hand, and likewise is sometimes not used with a cutting board at all, like when removing the skin from fruit.

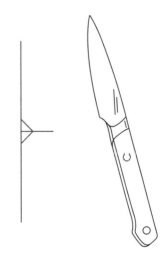

SERRATED KNIFE

A serrated knife is a knife with a long, narrow, jagged-tooth blade on one side. These teeth (of various designs) allow a serrated knife to cut through the exterior of a food without crushing or compacting its interior—best used for delicate foods like tomatoes, whose centers might be crushed when trying to cut through their skin with a regular knife, or tough-on-the-outside foods like winter squash, pineapples, or bread. Unlike other types of knives, where the motion of use might be rocking or pushing, a serrated knife works by sawing back and forth, so it is best for precision slicing, not for chopping or mincing. Sometimes the handle is offset from the blade in order to prevent the user's knuckles from coming into contact with the cutting surface; this is especially true in a common subtype of serrated knife, the bread knife.

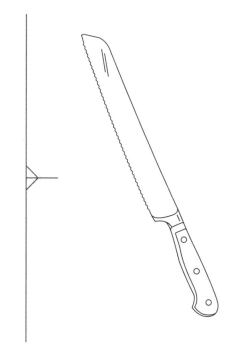

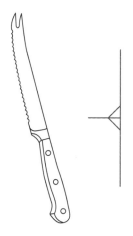

TOMATO KNIFE

With a small serrated blade, a tomato knife is meant to slice only tomatoes, cutting through the tough skin without crushing the delicate fruit's flesh. Some designs have a forked end, helpful in picking up finished slices for serving. The best substitution for a tomato knife is simply a serrated knife.

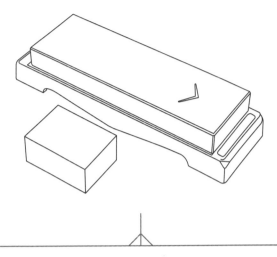

WHETSTONE

A whetstone, also called a sharpening stone, is a double-sided, textured stone or block used to sharpen a knife's blade. With each stroke of a knife across a whetstone, a small amount of metal is ground off to sharpen the knife's blade. To use a whetstone one is required to repeatedly run the length of the knife's edge against the stone at a shallow angle (usually 15 to 20 degrees) while applying light pressure to wear down a new edge. (This process also hones the blade straight, though a honing steel should be used when the blade is already sharp but just needs realignment.) Though it may be used dry, a whetstone can also be soaked in water or oil before use. The water or oil will hold some of the released grit from the blade and the whetstone in suspension, making less of a mess and creating an exfoliating slurry that helps with sharpening. The two sides of a whetstone usually have different textures, a coarser grit and a smoother grit. The coarse side is used first, to grind away any dings, burrs, or roughness that might be on the blade. One must be sure to run both sides of the blade, from handle to tip, across this side of the whetstone in order to ensure both sides of the blade have an equally smooth surface. Once the blade is appropriately buffed, the smoother side of the whetstone is then used. This side is used to sharpen the blade and polish the new edge; again, sharpening both sides of the blade is necessary. One of the benefits of using a whetstone is the ability to see and feel the sharpness of the edge as it is being created, which gives the user more control over the final product.

Ladles, Scoops & Spoons

Kitchens require many different utensils to move and manipulate food as it's being prepared, cooked, and served. This selection of tools shows the variety of ways things get picked up, scooped, stirred, drizzled, and more.

BASTER

A baster, also called a turkey baster, is a utensil that uses suction to take liquid from one place and deposit it elsewhere, often used to redeposit juices from a pan back onto the cooking item. Made of a long fat tube with a hollow squeezable bulb at one end, the baster works by squeezing the bulb prior to submerging in the liquid to be sucked up, releasing the bulb so suction draws the liquid into the tube, then squeezing the bulb again to eject the liquid onto its final location. A baster is convenient for grabbing liquids that are hard to spoon up, such as the cooking juices surrounding a roasting turkey; these liquids can then be squirted back onto the bird to moisten it. A baster can also be used to lift off the topmost layer of fat from a sauce, to separate liquids that have settled into layers by suctioning out only the parts you desire, or to transfer liquids from one place to another.

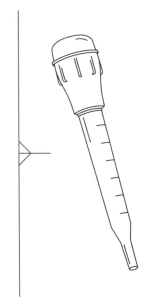

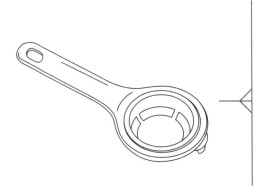

EGG SEPARATOR

An egg separator is a simple tool to aid in parting the raw egg white from the raw egg yolk. Similar to a slotted spoon (page 242), a separator looks like a deep plastic spoon with slots in the bowl; when one places a whole egg on it, the yolk is held back by the spoon and the whites drain through the slots. A thick-gauge wire spiral in the shape of a spoon's bowl (with a handle and a hook for hanging over the side of a bowl) is another style, which functions the same.

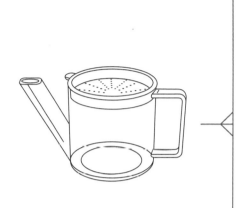

FAT SEPARATOR

A fat separator is a vessel with a handle and a long pouring spout attached to the bottom; its purpose is to isolate liquid fat from other liquids in a sauce, stock, or soup. The fat separator relies on the fact that fat rises to the top of other liquids. When a sauce to be degreased is added to the separator and given a few minutes to settle, the juices drift to the bottom and the grease floats to the top; because the spout is drawing from the bottom of the vessel, one can then carefully pour the juices into another container, stopping the pour before reaching the grease layer. The fat separator should be made of heatproof material like heavy glass or plastic, as the liquids added are often hot; it should also be transparent, so one can see when to stop pouring.

HONEY DIPPER

A honey dipper is a short wooden utensil, made up of a handle with a heavily grooved bulb-shape on one end. It is exclusively used for transferring honey from its pot or container to the desired destination, where it can be drizzled into tea or onto toast, for example. By dipping it into the pot, the grooved bulb effectively and easily collects a portion of honey, given its high-surface area. To keep the honey from dripping off the dipper, one slowly twirls the handle to counteract gravity's pull. A honey dipper is considered the best way to serve honey, as a neat drizzle disperses and dissolves better than a spoonful.

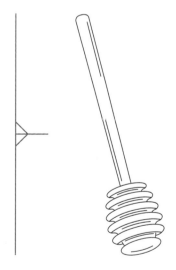

ICE CREAM SCOOP

An ice cream scoop is a specialized type of scoop used specifically for portioning and serving ice cream, frozen yogurt, or sorbet. The simplest ice cream scoop functions like a heavy spoon, with either a curving bowl shape or a straighter spade-like bowl shape, ideal for dipping into a large vat of ice cream. There are also curved ice cream scoops with spring-loaded handles that actively release the ice cream from the bowl, which portion out uniformly round portions. Most ice cream scoops are made from a metal that will prevent the ice cream from freezing to the scoop. An ice cream scoop may also be used to evenly portion other items besides ice cream, such as muffin or cupcake batter.

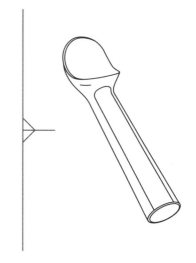

LADLE

A ladle, a utensil that functions as both a spoon and a scoop at the same time, is used to portion and serve liquid foods such as sauces, soups, and stews. Ladles have very long handles and a deep spherical bowl to hold the food, which makes it easier to reach into deep stock pots. Ladles in professional kitchens have bowls that are measured in ounces for easy uniformity, convenient when portioning batter or adding oil to a wok.

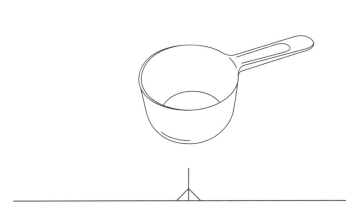

MIXING SPOON

A mixing spoon is a large spoon with a long handle and shallow bowl, made from a variety of materials including metal, plastic, or wood. It is specifically intended for kitchen use, either for mixing or blending ingredients together, or for stirring ingredients that have already been mixed, like when cooking something on the stovetop. While most mixing spoons have an intact bowl, some have slots or holes, depending on its use.

SCOOP

The scoop is a utensil used to portion and/or move food, depending on its type. A measuring scoop or cup, with its short handle and simple bowl (often shaped similarly to a teacup), is used for measuring and transferring dry ingredients like flour and sugar. Most often, they hold amounts as small as ¼ cup, up to 2 cups. One uses a measuring scoop by dipping it into the dry goods, then leveling off the top with a straight edge or knife. There are also rounded measured scoops, called disher scoops, with a mechanism that releases the scooped food cleanly from the vessel by the user clenching a spring-loaded handle. These are more common in professional kitchens, and are named to indicate how many level scoops it will take to fill a 32-ounce container: it will take 4 scoops for a #4 scoop to fill a 32-ounce container, it will take 100 scoops for a #100 scoop to fill the same container. These are used for portioning, like with cookie dough, and serving, like with ice cream. There is also a scoop shaped like a shovel, which does not provide exact measurements but is usually used to transfer dry goods from large containers to smaller ones.

SERVING SPOON

A serving spoon is a large spoon used for distributing individual portions of food from a shared bowl or platter. It usually has a slightly longer handle than a regular spoon, which is intended to make it easier to serve from dishes of any depth. Serving spoons can be found in sets of flatware, along with a serving fork and/or slotted spoon, or can be a one-off piece, made from a variety of materials.

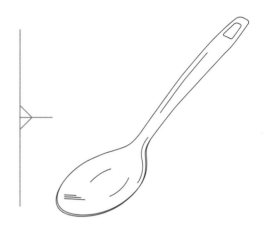

SKIMMER

Similar to a spider (page 244), a skimmer is a tool that one uses to lift foods away from a hot liquid, as in deep-frying or when blanching. It includes a very long handle, good for keeping a safe distance from the hot oil or water. The bowl of the skimmer can be designed in a variety of different materials, the most common being mesh, for very fine skimming (like removing food particles from frying oil). Slots or perforations cut into a silicone or metal bowl is another popular design, which is best used for lifting out larger chunks of food from a pot of oil or water, thereby letting the oil or water drain away.

SLOTTED SPOON

A slotted spoon has holes or slots in the bowl of the spoon that enables solid foods to be lifted away from liquids. Functionally, it can be a cooking utensil, where it would be used to drain foods, like cubes of meat from the grease left in the pan, or it can be a serving utensil, for watery, saucy, or greasy foods where one wants to control the amount of liquid served, like with cooked greens. The slots in serving spoons take on a variety of different shapes and sizes depending on style or their end use.

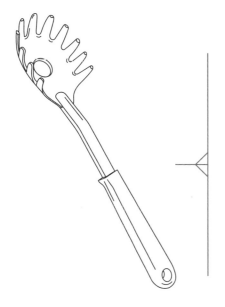

SPAGHETTI SPOON

A single-use utensil, the spaghetti spoon is used only to remove cooked spaghetti from a pot of boiling water and to serve it. Despite its lack of range, it remains a very popular kitchen utensil, perhaps due to its inclusion in most kitchen tool multipacks. It has a long handle and a deep concave bowl with a single large hole or multiple smaller holes, and finger-like prongs emanating from the edge of the bowl to capture the strands of pasta. The spaghetti spoon's clawlike shape does stir, separate, and grab spaghetti and other long pastas well, but multipurpose tongs will do the job just as easily.

Pasta Overload

Perhaps to create the perception of additional value for an otherwise replaceable utensil, some people have stated that the hole in the middle of a spaghetti spoon can also measure a single serving of uncooked spaghetti. Unfortunately for them, the shape and size of the hole varies from brand to brand, so this is not a consistent or reliable method of counting servings.

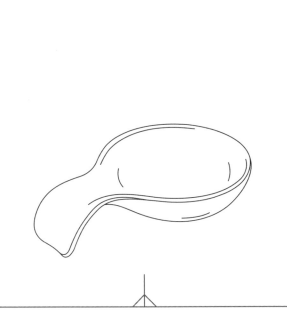

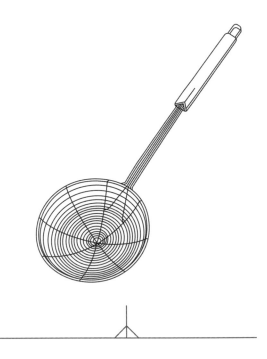

SPOON REST

A spoon rest is a shallow physical barrier used to temporarily hold a kitchen tool when it is not in active use, like a wooden spoon being used to stir a stew. Similar in purpose to a coaster (page 138) or a chopstick rest (page 153), a spoon rest serves two purposes. First, a spoon rest prevents juices or cooking liquids clinging to the spoon from dirtying the kitchen counters. Second, the rest keeps the spoon itself from becoming contaminated by other kitchen surfaces, which could have come into contact with raw meat or soapy water, for example. The rest itself comes in a wide variety of sizes, shapes, and decorations, and can be made of all sorts of materials, ranging from wood and ceramic to plastic and metal. Though called a spoon rest, this tool may be used for resting all sorts of kitchen implements that are used to stir or manipulate food in a pot, pan, or bowl, such as a set of tongs (page 255) or an eggbeater (page 208).

SPIDER

Similar to a skimmer (page 242), a spider functions like a colander with a handle, easily lifting foods out of hot liquids like oil or water. A spider is the best tool for retrieving cooked short pasta from a pot to put directly into a pan of sauce, or removing finished French fries from hot oil. Its long handle helps distance the cook from splatters, and its wire, bowl-shaped head is wide enough to capture a lot of food when every second counts (as in blanching and frying) yet minimal enough to not lower the temperature of the liquid. Best of all, the wide gauge of the wires in the bowl of the spider means that each sweep with it will drain immediately, so that no time will be wasted lingering over the pot, waiting for liquid to drip back into it.

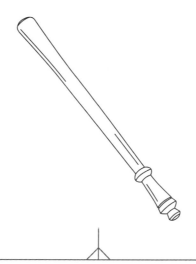

SPURTLE

A spurtle is a Scottish kitchen tool used for stirring porridge as it cooks in a pot on the stovetop. Porridge made from oatmeal—the old-fashioned, steel-cut kind, which takes much longer to cook than the rolled or instant version—has a tendency to stick to the bottom of the pan and can become lumpy unless it is stirred continuously. Stirring oatmeal as it cooks also makes the porridge creamier, as some of the excess starch is released, thickening the cooking liquid (much like stirring rice in a risotto). The spurtle is intended to combat these problems more directly than a regular wooden spoon, as it agitates the oats easily without incorporating any excess air and gently scrapes the sides, corners, and bottom of the pot, thereby ensuring that its contents won't burn or stick. The ease of use, since a spurtle causes little drag, also means that the cook can stir continuously without too much effort. The Scottish version, which has been in existence since at least the fifteenth century, consists of a simple, rod-shaped dowel ranging in diameter from a ½ inch to 1½ inches, and often features carved details or knobs on the top end. The bottom of the tool has a blunted tip that may be tapered or bulb-shaped, and it is made of either carved or turned wood. There is an American version of this tool, which is shaped like a tall and narrow paddle. This version may be used for agitating oats as well as folding batters and stirring stews and since it is also made of wood, it can be helpful for scooping or scraping food out of nonstick pots and pans.

Spurtle Experts

———————◯———————

Spurtles may feel somewhat exotic to non-Scots, but in their home country they are a common kitchen tool. After all, Scotland is a place that loves its oats, so much so that there is an annual festival dedicated to the spurtle and the oatmeal it helps create: The Golden Spurtle World Porridge Making Championship. The championship's main attraction is a contest where participants are asked to make the smoothest, creamiest porridge they can in a small amount of time. After judges deliberate, the winner receives the Golden Spurtle trophy. Specialty porridge is another growing contest category, where unusual oatmeal recipes go head-to-head.

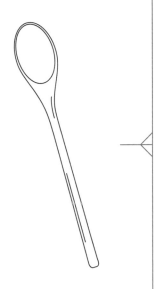

WOODEN SPOON

One of the most classic and multipurpose tools in the kitchen, the wooden spoon is the best tool for mixing dry or wet ingredients, or for tossing items being sautéed in a pan. Strong yet lightweight, it is equally effective at difficult work like beating together stiff ingredients, such as a cookie dough, or easy jobs like stirring a brothy soup. Because it is made from wood, this spoon is safe to use in any pot, as wood will not scratch stainless steel, nonstick, or enamel pans. Plus its wooden handle does not conduct heat, so it will stay cool even if resting on top of a hot pan or pot. Most commonly, it's constructed from a single piece of wood, and consists of a long handle and a shallow oval bowl; however they can also have a flat edge, which is convenient for times when you are deglazing a pan or stirring something that will stick to the bottom of a pot, like a risotto.

Alternative Uses for a Wooden Spoon

A wooden spoon is already multipurpose, but there are a few untraditional ways in which to use this commonplace utensil. The handle end of the spoon can be used to test the general temperature of oil—just hold the tip of the spoon upside down in the oil in a pan—the smaller and faster the oil bubbles around the wood, the hotter it is (and if not bubbling at all, it is not yet hot). A spoon laid across a pot of ingredients blanching in water can help it from foaming over, as it will break the surface tension. And lastly, wooden spoons make a classic baby toy, excellent for banging on an upside-down pot.

Tongs, Paddles & Spatulas

This collection of flat-headed tools is used primarily to move and shape ingredients. From flipping a burger on a grill to swirling frosting onto a cake, these utensils are vital for manipulating food as it is being cooked and assembled.

BUTTER PADDLES

Always sold in a set of two, butter paddles are identical wooden blades with short handles, about the size of a set of hands. The paddles are used to work churned butter directly after it is made, processing and shaping it without warming the butter via the heat of one's hands. The narrow vertical ridges on the face of each blade are meant for wicking away excess buttermilk as the butter is kneaded; removing as much of this liquid as possible is necessary for keeping butter fresh for longer. The paddles can also be used to thoroughly mix salt (if preferred) into the finished butter and to mold the butter into a form, giving a distinctive ribbed texture to the exterior.

Butter in All Forms

Historically, churning one's own butter was a common practice which meant more people were exposed to the conundrum of deciding what form their finished butter should take. Shaping butter into a simple block for cooking and kitchen use was a common solution, and butter paddles were often used to press it into shape, which could create a ribbed texture on the butter block's exterior. Then, when butter was eaten at the table, a butter curler (page 196) could be wielded on the larger block to create individual curls for serving. Decorative stamps and molds offered popular shaping alternatives, impressing images of flowers, leaves, shells, fruit, and more, directly onto the butter. This personalization through decoration was especially helpful to those who sold their butter to the wider community, as it allowed their butter to be identified and traced back to its maker. On the more extreme end of the butter shaping spectrum, sculpting with butter has a storied history, though obviously this mode of forming churned butter is practiced less for personal use and focuses more on shaping butter for public or promoted displays, such as state fairs. This makes sense, as creating a bust of a political figure, a full statue, or a historical scene out of butter requires refrigeration on a large scale as well as specialized tools that go way beyond what any regular kitchen will include.

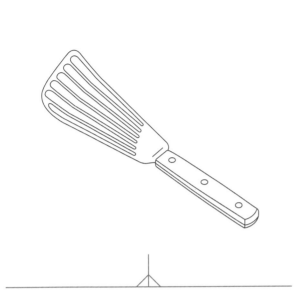

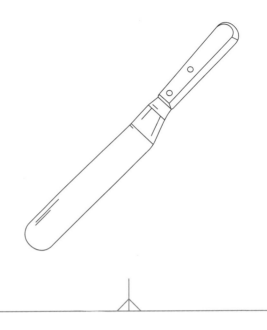

FISH SPATULA

The fish spatula is a special type of spatula that is designed specifically to lift and flip fish fillets, though it can be used with other delicate foods as well. While a regular slotted spatula has a relatively short and rigid metal head with a few slots cut into it, the fish spatula is wide and slightly curved, with thinner slats and much larger slots; its overall design is lighter, more flexible, less obtrusive, and less cumbersome, making it easier to slide nimbly under a fragile fillet without much disturbance. Because it has a wider flat surface than a regular spatula, it works especially well for flipping longer foods, like rustic slices of bread in French toast or a grilled sandwich. In addition to its uses in the kitchen, it also makes a good serving tool, as its minimal profile means less drag on the food when you are sliding underneath it.

OFFSET SPATULA

An offset spatula, sometimes called an icing spatula, is a metal spatula with a long narrow blade—ranging from narrow to wide—and a blunted end that is set at a lower level than its handle, hence the name *offset*. The purpose of the offset spatula, available in a variety of sizes, is to flip ingredients and to apply, spread, and smooth batters, fillings, frostings, and icings. The reason for the offset design is to make the tool easy to use without one's hand getting in the way (a straight spatula, page 254, does not have this feature). Smaller offset spatulas are best for icing cookies, while the larger options are best for frosting cakes or flipping burgers. Because its blade is somewhat flexible, an offset spatula is also useful for other kitchen jobs, like prying stuck baked items out of pans or sliding under delicate cookies to flip them or transfer them to a rack.

PIZZA PEEL

Like a flattened shovel or a giant spatula (page 254), a pizza peel (also called a baking peel) is a large utensil meant for moving whole uncooked and cooked pizzas in and out of a pizza oven. Usually made of wood, bamboo, or aluminum, a standard pizza peel comes with a long handle (measuring up to a couple feet long) and a thin, rigid, paddle-like surface at one end. The paddle or spatula-like portion of the pizza peel must be flat and nimble enough to slide between the prep surface and the topped, uncooked pizza dough, or between the finished pizza and the pizza oven floor or stone (page 54) in order to transport the pizza; dusting the peel with flour or cornmeal helps to prevent any sticking. Not often found in home kitchens, a pizza peel is a must-have tool in pizzerias and restaurant settings. However, with the proliferation of residential outdoor pizza ovens, a pizza peel would be a worthwhile investment for pizza fanatics.

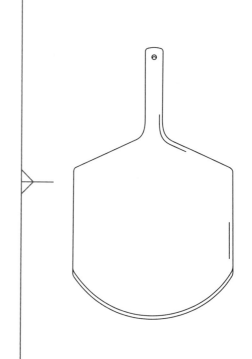

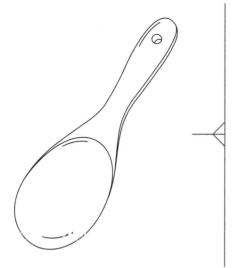

RICE PADDLE

A rice paddle, also called a *shamoji* in Japanese, is a special utensil made specifically for mixing, folding, and serving cooked sushi rice. A cross between a spatula and a spoon, the paddle's head is flat with a rounded edge, and is attached to a short handle; the paddle is a touch larger than most serving spoons. Often made of wood, bamboo, or plastic, a rice paddle is sometimes included with a rice cooker. The rice paddle is especially adept at thoroughly mixing cooked rice with a salty and sweet vinegar mixture to create seasoned sushi rice; the paddle's shape makes it ideal for gently folding and aerating the rice without breaking it.

The Ultimate Kitchen Tool

One could easily argue that the best, most convenient kitchen tools available do not have an entry in this book. These tools are easy to use, easy to clean, and don't cost anything. They are impossible to find at a garage sale, and won't be found on any wedding registry, or via any online retailers because they are . . . a pair of hands. Cliché but true, one's own two hands truly are the best tools for tossing, spreading, juicing, stretching, squeezing, grabbing, and flipping, to name just a few tasks related to food preparation and cooking that are easily performed by a pair of (well-washed) hands. Although they are not resistant to heat or cold (though some chefs might argue they have "asbestos hands" and are therefore able to touch very hot things), hands can accomplish quite a bit, and without them cooking would likely be impossible.

SPATULA

A spatula is a multipurpose kitchen utensil used for flipping foods during cooking as well as lifting cooked foods off a pan or baking sheet. It has a long handle and a rectangular flat surface for a head, thin enough to slide underneath foods such as pancakes, cookies, fried eggs, or burgers. A spatula needs to be rigid enough to be able to lift the food for flipping or serving; some are still a bit flexible so as not to crush the food when it's sliding beneath it. The head of a spatula is usually made from metal or plastic, and can be slotted or solid.

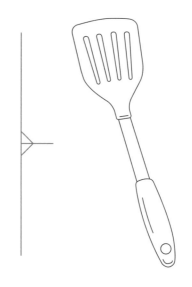

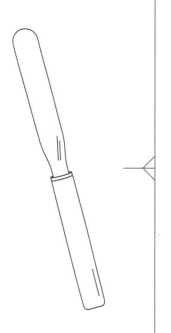

STRAIGHT SPATULA

Similar to a palette knife with a rounded tip, a straight spatula is a thin, flexible strip of metal that has no sharp edges and is attached to a handle. The straight spatula goes by a variety of names, from cake spatula, icing spatula, or frosting spatula to a flat spatula or spreader, but all perform the same basic function. Often used for cake and cookie decoration, the straight spatula is a convenient utensil for applying, spreading, and smoothing frostings, icings, and other loose-textured foods. Sizes vary, with large straight spatulas used for decorating cakes and smaller options used for decorating cookies. In addition to decorating needs, straight spatulas can be helpful in loosening and removing lasagna, breads, or other baked goods from a pan or tray, both by cutting them away from a pan's edge and by providing leverage for wrestling them out of a dish. The offset spatula (page 251) offers a slight variation on this tool by featuring a blade and handle that are on slightly different planes rather than occurring in one straight line.

Cake Decorating 101

Frosting a cake requires practice and expertise, as well as a handful of tools and tricks. To start, be sure that the cake is cool (a hot cake will melt the frosting), and the frosting is room temperature. Placing the cake on a turntable (page 98) to decorate will make it easier to create a smooth finish, but know that it will likely have to be transferred to a plate or cake stand (page 170) before serving. Use a straight or offset spatula to apply a very thin coating of frosting to the assembled cake layers, and chill: this coat locks any errant crumbs from the trimmed cakes in suspension and prevents them from mixing with the final layer of frosting. Finally, spread frosting on the top of the assembled cake using a spatula; follow with the sides, holding the spatula vertically and spinning the turntable, or by moving the spatula around the perimeter of the cake.

If there are air bubbles in the frosting, dip the spatula into hot water and dry, then apply it to the surface of the frosted cake for a final spin: the heat will melt the exterior frosting slightly and create a smooth finish. Once a smooth layer of icing is achieved, add other decorations using a pastry bag (page 182) and pastry tips (page 183).

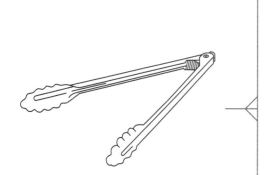

TONGS

With their two long, connected or spring-loaded arms, tongs are used to grab and lift food single-handedly. The end of the arms range in finishes and styles, from simple all-metal versions with scalloped metal "hands," to versions that are silicone-dipped for a softer grip. The arms themselves can be short or long—extra-long ones are marketed especially for grilling—to keep one's hands away from the heat. As opposed to a spatula or spoon, tongs are able to grab onto food, so can be helpful in situations where food is slippery (like spaghetti), in pieces (like salad), or heavy (like a roast). They are also more precise, making them the best tool for flipping or arranging things in a pan or on a grill. Some smaller tongs are created specifically for serving sugar cubes and ice.

Sharp Tools

BENCH SCRAPER

BISCUIT CUTTER

CHEESE CUTTER

CHITARRA

COOKIE CUTTER

EGG SLICER

LAME

MANDOLINE

MINCER

PASTRY BLENDER

PASTRY WHEEL

PEELER

PIE CUTTER

PIZZA SLICER

POULTRY SHEARS

RAVIOLI CUTTER/STAMP

SHEARS

SKEWER

SPIRALIZER

TOOTHPICK

TRUSSING NEEDLE

In cooking, there are sharp tools other than knives made especially for cutting, shredding, stamping, and skewering. While many of these could in theory be replaced by a sharp paring knife (page 233), the consistency and ease and speed of use would be hard to duplicate.

BENCH SCRAPER

A bench scraper is a simple wide flat rectangular blade, with a dull edge on one long side and a handle attached to the opposite side. Best for cutting only very soft things, the bench scraper is convenient for portioning ground meat or doughs, and is typically etched with ruler measurements for precision, as it is often used in baking. As indicated by its name, the bench scraper is also helpful for scraping clean the "bench," i.e. the cutting board. Similarly, it is good for transferring prepped ingredients like herbs or vegetables from the cutting board to the pan, by sweeping them onto the flat side of the blade. Like a cleaver (page 229), its flat surface can also be used to smash ingredients like garlic and ginger.

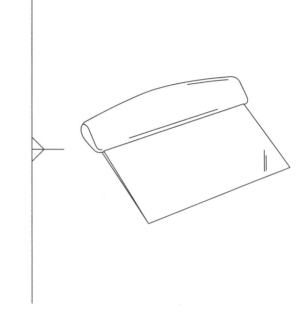

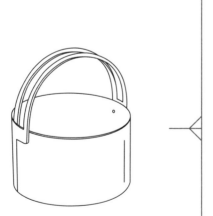

BISCUIT CUTTER

A biscuit cutter is a tin, stainless steel, or plastic hand tool that punches out shapes from a sheet of dough to make (American-style) biscuits specifically. The difference between it and a cookie cutter (page 260) is mostly due to the height of the straight sides, which are taller on a biscuit cutter to accommodate thicker dough. Usually round, but occasionally rectangular or polygonal, the sides of a biscuit cutter are either flat or fluted, and sometimes come with an arching handle at the top for ease of use. It is tempting to substitute other kitchen items for a biscuit cutter (like a drinking glass), but without the sharp edge that a cutter has, the biscuits risk having their carefully constructed layers crushed and their height stunted.

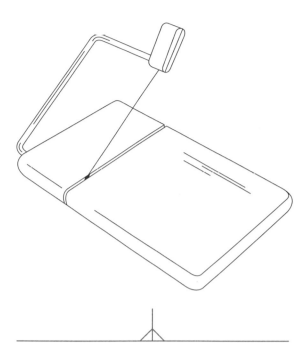

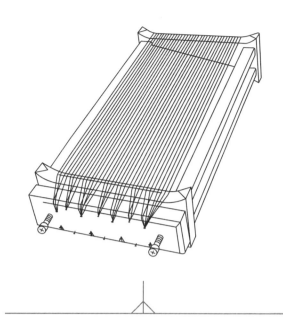

CHEESE CUTTER

A cheese cutter slices or divides cheese that could be crushed by the weight and pressure of a knife; instead, a cheese cutter uses a taut wire to make a clean cut. There are two common designs: a wire with a handle on either end, which one holds at tension and presses into the cheese to create a clean slice; or a board with a suspended wire attached, which one swings down on a lever through the block of cheese. The wire is made of a very fine metal such as stainless steel or aluminum, and the handles are often made from wood or plastic; the board is usually marble, metal, wood, or plastic. A cheese cutter is used in professional or retail kitchens, for consistent and efficient cutting of large amounts of cheese into smaller portions.

CHITARRA

A type of pasta cutter, the *chitarra* (from the Italian for guitar) is a mechanical tool used to cut fresh pasta sheets into skinny rectangular strands. The guitar reference is due to this tool's visual appearance and design: a chitarra consists of multiple parallel wires strung tightly across a simple wooden frame. The taut wires are made of thin stainless steel and are typically only a couple of millimeters apart. To use, one forces the sheet of pasta on top of and through the strings with a specially made rolling pin, cutting the pasta into squared strands.

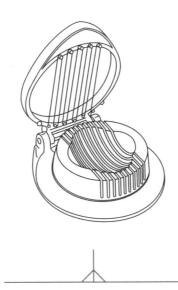

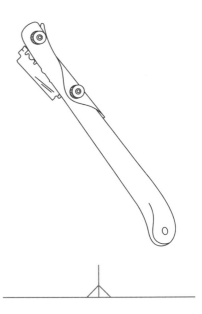

COOKIE CUTTER

Similar to a biscuit cutter (page 258), cookie cutters are sharp edged stamps that are able to cut shapes out of cookie or pastry dough. Made of stainless steel, tin, or plastic, cookie cutters come in a wide variety of sizes and shapes, from time-tested stars, circles, and people (think gingerbread men and women), to more esoteric designs of animals and letters. Though use of the term "cookie cutter" in daily conversation can be derogatory—as an identifier of homogeneity—when used for baking, cookie cutters provide helpful uniformity, especially for commercial bakeries.

EGG SLICER

An egg slicer is a simple device used to evenly slice or chop a peeled hard-boiled egg. With a slotted molded stand to hold the egg and a hinged frame with multiple thin parallel cutting wires, the tool functions by pressing the wires through the egg, effectively slicing the egg. To chop the egg, carefully spin the sliced egg 90 degrees and cut one or two more times. The egg slicer can work with other soft foods, like mushrooms and strawberries.

LAME

Consisting of a small, curved razor blade mounted to a small handle, a lame is a bread baking tool used to create shallow cuts or flaps in dough after its final round of proofing and directly prior to baking. These slashes provide both a release for excess steam by creating a vent through the dough's "skin," as well as a predetermined location for weak spots where the yeasted loaf will expand in the heat of the oven. Most bakers like to control these weak spots as they can have an impact on the final look of the loaf or bun.

Bread Slashing

In addition to the technical necessity of slashing dough, the scores created by a lame provide an opportunity to brand each loaf in the "signature" of its creator, as the choice in placement of these bold slashes can be particular to each baker, and even each type of bread. As the exterior of a shaped piece of dough is often lightly dusted in white flour, the slashes result in high-contrasting brown markings after baking is done, since the undusted interior dough becomes exposed when allowed to bloom in the oven. In this sense, slashing loaves both identifies the baker and can also visually differentiate one flavor of bread from another, as the baker can slash all of one type of bread with a particular set of marks, and use another mark for a different type.

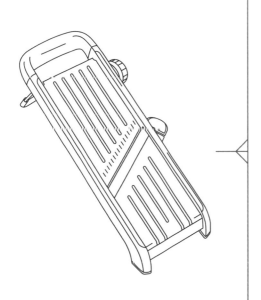

MANDOLINE

A mandoline is a kitchen tool used for slicing or shredding to create uniform pieces of hard foods, such as potatoes for chips. Most commonly consisting of a mounted horizontal blade—which can be straight, v-shaped, or wavy—the mandoline is used by pushing the food across the blade while applying force, so that a slice is shaved off. The distance between the blade and the mounting, which is usually adjustable, determines the thickness of the slice. Because of the force needed and the proximity of one's hand to the blade, mandolines are notoriously dangerous; some models come with a guard that sits on top of the food being sliced to create a barrier between one's hand and the blade. Some mandolines also come with specialized attachments to create julienne, crinkle cuts, or waffle cuts.

MINCER

Like a hybrid between a mezzaluna (page 233) and a pizza slicer (page 264), the mincer is a hand-held device with multiple parallel circular blades, used to mince herbs and other small foods. By rolling the sharp blades of the mincer back and forth across the food on a cutting board, one can quickly break it down.

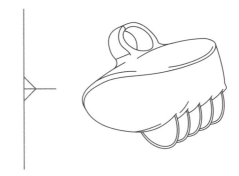

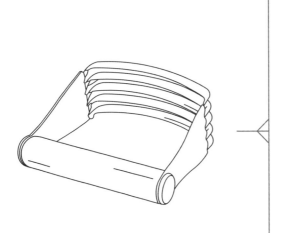

PASTRY BLENDER

With a heavy-duty horizontal handle and multiple rounded tines that loop from one end of the handle to the other, a pastry blender (also known as a pastry cutter) is a must-have when incorporating butter or shortening into a pastry dough's dry ingredients. This stout instrument is meant to cut the fat into the flour so that each piece is small but distinct, and coated in flour, which helps make the final pastry flaky. While purists might make the case for performing this act by hand, smearing each piece of butter between one's fingers and tossing it in the flour, the pastry blender has the important benefit of being cooler than the average human body temperature, which helps keep the butter from melting.

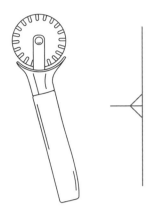

PASTRY WHEEL

Like a smaller scale pizza slicer (page 264), a pastry wheel is a circular-bladed hand tool that is used to cut rolled-out pastry, pasta, and other doughs. Most pastry wheels include either a straight blade or a fluted blade, and are used to create a decorative edge. Some models are double-headed, allowing for the inclusion of both straight and fluted blade designs.

PEELER

A peeler, also known as a swivel peeler or vegetable peeler, is a common kitchen gadget used to remove the outside layer of a food, often the peels of fruits or vegetables, by stroking the peeler against the outside of the food with some force. Most peelers have a plastic or stainless-steel handle holding the slot blade straight; versions that feature perpendicular blades are called Y peelers. A serrated peeler has a serrated blade, best used for softer foods like peppers and tomatoes, and a julienne peeler has a blade that creates thin strips with every stroke.

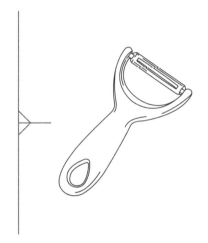

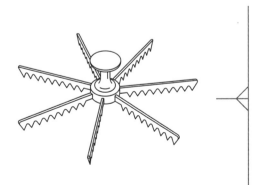

PIE CUTTER

Similar to an apple cutter but on a much larger scale, a pie cutter is a multi-bladed stamp that evenly divides a pie into ready-to-serve slices. By pressing the pie cutter down on a whole baked pie, the rigid blades neatly cut through to the bottom crust. Used primarily in commercial and restaurant kitchens, a pie cutter comes in multiple sizes and will cut a pie into four or more wedges, depending on the number of blades.

PIZZA SLICER

A pizza slicer cuts a whole pizza into individual pieces, often triangles or squares. The most common design is a sharp, small wheel-shaped blade attached to a handle; one rolls it across a pizza in a straight line to cut through the bottom crust and toppings. Another style of pizza cutter consists of a very long curved blade with a handle on each end, similar to a mezzaluna (page 233) but longer. Used more frequently in restaurants and pizza parlors, this style of pizza cutter is rocked across a cooked pizza to halve the pizza, then again to create individual slices.

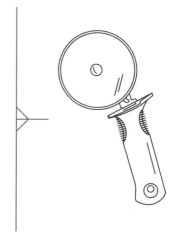

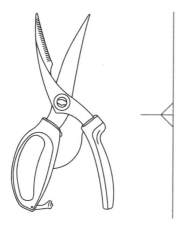

POULTRY SHEARS

Poultry shears are intended, obviously, to cut poultry—both cutting through bone and snipping through skin—so they are more heavy-duty and substantial than regular shears. Because of the job they need to do, they are most often spring loaded to help power through each cut. Unlike shears, which have two looped handles, poultry shears often have one looped handle and one straight handle. Most models separate into two pieces for easy cleaning.

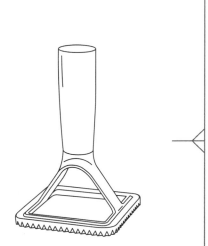

RAVIOLI CUTTER/STAMP

A ravioli cutter, or ravioli stamp, is used to cut individual ravioli out of a sheet of fresh pasta. Consisting of a short, vertical piece of rigid metal formed into a circle or square shape and attached to a wooden, metal, or plastic handle that arches over, some ravioli cutters also feature fluted edges that provide an added level of decoration. There are a few ways to use the cutter, but the most popular way begins by laying a fresh pasta sheet on top of a floured surface. Then, dollops of filling are placed evenly across the sheet, leaving an inch or two of space between each dollop. Next, the dough surrounding each of the mounds of filling is lightly moistened with water using a pastry brush (page 183) or a finger, then the entire sheet is topped with another sheet of fresh pasta. To seal each mound of filling between the two sheets of dough, press the two sheets together between and around each mound of filling, carefully expelling as much air as possible. The ravioli cutter is then employed to cut cleanly around each mound, through both layers of dough, creating a set of individual ravioli.

SHEARS

Shears are specially-designed kitchen scissors that are intended for cutting a wide variety of foods, such as herbs, leafy greens and vegetables, and meats and poultry. (See also poultry shears, page 264.) They can be small and delicate, best for precision work, or heavy duty and large, able to cut through meats (though poultry shears are best for large jobs). Many models of shears separate at the hinge to make them easier to clean, and some include additional design features such as bottle openers.

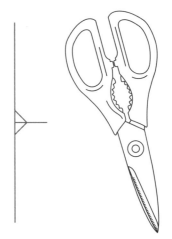

Shears As Tableware

In Korea, shears are sometimes used as a table utensil as well as a kitchen tool. As most food is eaten with chopsticks and spoons, not forks and knives, this sharp edge is a helpful addition to the table when things need to be reduced to bite size. Since they work without needing a cutting board or even two hands, shears are a practical, quick way to cut noodles, cooked meat, or savory pancakes into smaller pieces for easy eating.

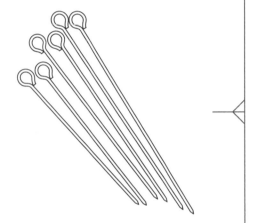

SKEWER

Usually thin rods with a single sharpened end and a looped end for handling, skewers are used both to spear food in preparation for cooking and to eat from directly. Skewers can be made of all sorts of materials, depending on their end use; even a toothpick (page 269) is a skewer of sorts. Bamboo skewers are multipurpose: if heavy duty, they can be soaked and used for grilling, as well as for skewering raw or already cooked foods for a special presentation. Metal skewers are common for grilling, where cooks spear chunks of meat, vegetables, or a combination of foods and place the loaded skewer over a fire to cook; raw ground meat can even be shaped directly around a skewer for cooking. Metal versions conduct some heat as well, so they are able to cook the food from the inside as well as from the direct heat from the grill. No matter the material, flat skewers are considered the easiest to use, as you can turn the food over for even cooking without the food spinning on its axel. Lastly, skewers can also be used for fastening foods that need securing before cooking, like the cavity of a stuffed turkey to be roasted or a filled pepper to be fried.

SPIRALIZER

With recent dieting trends including reducing one's carbohydrate consumption, the spiralizer, a manual or electric vegetable prep machine, has become increasingly prevalent. The device's name stems from its purpose: to create spiral-shaped pieces of raw hard vegetables. When a zucchini is run through a spiralizer, the resulting strands are commonly called "zoodles"—an amalgam of the words *zucchini* and *noodles*. Indeed, spiralized vegetables of all kinds often stand in for pasta: briefly blanched or sautéed, they can retain an al dente-like bite that will not fool a pasta eater, but will provide a nutritious bed for pasta sauces of all kinds. Spiralized vegetables can also be eaten raw in salads and side dishes, making otherwise unpalatable-when-raw vegetables (like butternut squash or beets) deliciously consumable. The machine works in a variety of ways, but most screw the vegetable onto a set of blades like a pencil sharpener, forcing it through by turning the blades, the vegetable, or a crank. The result is ribbon- or strand-like curls of raw vegetables, in a variety of different thicknesses and shapes depending on the design of the blades.

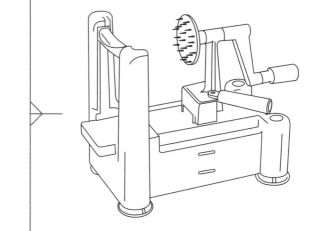

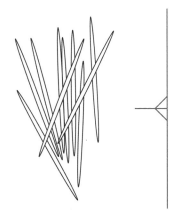

TOOTHPICK

A toothpick is a very small skewer-like utensil most commonly used as either a serving mechanism for small single bites of food, often appetizers or passed hors d'oerves, or as a tool for dislodging food that is stuck in one's teeth. These days most toothpicks are disposable and made from birch wood or plastic, but antique silver or metal versions certainly exist. Toothpicks are also utilized as a method of securing a piece of food to be cooked, like wrapping bacon around a raw scallop or pinning closed the opening of a stuffed vegetable or meat.

TRUSSING NEEDLE

An old-fashioned tool, a trussing needle—a long, heavy-gauge needle used with kitchen twine—is used to tie up poultry in preparation for cooking. When untrussed, a bird might cook unevenly, as the open cavity will fill with hot air, cooking parts of the bird from the inside; by trussing the bird into a single bundled shape, that cavity will be closed and the more uniform shape will produce more even cooking. Trussing has fallen a bit out of fashion, but if called for, a trussing needle will make the job easier; however, it is not always necessary—kitchen twine tied around the outside of the bird is most often adequate.

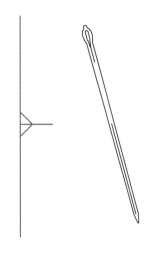

Whisks

BALL WHISK

BALLOON WHISK

DOUGH WHISK

FLAT WHISK

FRENCH WHISK

At its most basic, a whisk is a collection of wires used for mixing and whipping ingredients. With various configurations of coils, each type of whisk has a particular specialty, whether to incorporate air, to emulsify, or to eliminate lumps, among other tasks. The more wires the whisk has, the quicker you can accomplish your task. If space is at a premium, a French whisk will accomplish most undertakings competently; having others in your collection will make specialized jobs easier and faster. Note too that the motion you create with your whisk will also have an effect on a whisk's abilities: An up and down or cyclical motion will incorporate more air into your ingredients (best for beating eggs or whipping cream), and a side to side motion will incorporate less air, so bear this in mind depending on how light you would like your ingredients to be.

BALL WHISK

The ball whisk is a less common whisk, constructed of multiple straight, stiff wires each topped with a small metal ball. It is best used as a mixing and emulsifying tool, ideal for mixing dressings and dry ingredients. Its long tines and concentrated focus makes reaching corners easy, so every ingredient, even those at the bottom of a cup or curve of a bowl or pot, will be fully incorporated. Its shape is especially conducive to working in smaller vessels like a measuring cup, where even a narrow French whisk will not fit.

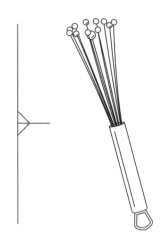

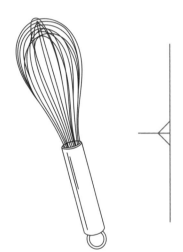

BALLOON WHISK

The balloon whisk is the most common whisk, and has thin wires curved into a round shape. As with all whisks, it can thoroughly combine disparate ingredients, whether wet or dry. But its relatively large size—as compared to other whisks— and bulbous shape make it ideal for incorporating air into an ingredient. It is the best tool to reach for when whipping egg whites or cream, or lightening a batter.

DOUGH WHISK

The dough whisk's esoteric shape—a flat circle of wire with two smaller loops twisted inside—is specifically made for blending batters and doughs without overworking the ingredients. The many tines of a regular whisk would overdevelop the gluten of a bread dough, for example, making it tough, but the dough whisk—also called a Danish whisk—breaks up unmixed pockets of ingredients with less agitation. Also, a dough whisk's simpler design won't trap ingredients like a regular whisk. The thicker wire easily scrapes the sides of the mixing bowl and cuts through stiff batters.

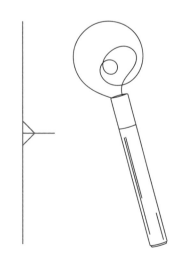

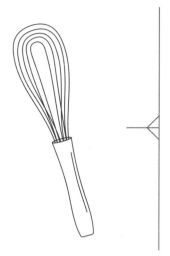

FLAT WHISK

The flat whisk is used primarily for emulsifying and blending pastes and sauces that are made in a pan. While any whisk could in theory be used for these tasks, the flat whisk's more two-dimensional shape covers more of the pan's surface area at once, blending its ingredients faster and more thoroughly. A flat whisk is ideal for making a roux, deglazing pans, incorporating liquids into a sauce, and smoothing out lumps in a cooked sauce like a béchamel. If using a nonstick pan, a silicone or wooden flat whisk won't scratch the pan's surface; otherwise, stick with the usual stainless-steel varieties.

FRENCH WHISK

The French whisk is a narrow, tapered whisk with thicker wires. Since it comes in a variety of sizes and has a very sturdy structure, the French whisk is the most multipurpose of all of the whisks. It can incorporate air into a mixture (though not as quickly as a balloon whisk), and is best used for stirring and blending.

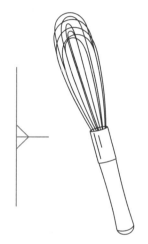

Julia Child

Julia Child is often credited with popularizing the whisk with Americans after appearing with one on television in 1963. More straightforward than the mechanical eggbeater and more efficient than a fork, the whisk simplified many kitchen tasks. Further, whipping egg whites for a soufflé, cooking a roux, or deglazing a pan are all classic European culinary techniques that are best performed with a whisk, so one could argue the "arrival" of the whisk in the US helped the cuisines of Western Europe find a home on the other side of the Atlantic.

INDEX A TO Z

INDEX BY USAGE